INCLUDES MANY
20-MINUTES-FROM-GROCERY-BAG-TO-DINNER-TABLE RECIPES

# Help!

## MY FAMILY'S HUNGRY

# J U D I E   B Y R D

© 2001 Judie Byrd

ISBN 1-58660-302-7

Layout and typesetting by Robyn Martins and Gladys Dunlap

Illustrations by John Schreiner

Published by Promise Press, an imprint of Barbour Publishing, Inc., P.O. Box 719, Uhrichsville, Ohio 44683, http://www.promisepress.com

 Member of the
Evangelical Christian
Publishers Association

Printed in the United States of America.

*To Teresa, my daughter and best friend.*
*And to Stephanie, my idea of the perfect daughter-in-law.*

*A mere* thank-you does not begin to express my gratitude to those who helped me write this book. For thirty-seven years, my husband Bill has been my partner and encourager of all things culinary. How I appreciate his exuberance for all my experiments and concoctions and the way he makes me feel like the world's best cook, even when a new idea turns out "less than desirable"! He is the "business end" of all my projects and is always willing to work on my ideas and plans. "Making ideas happen" wouldn't happen without him!

I am fortunate to have raised three foodies. I was able to try new recipes and dishes, and I always knew they would at least try whatever I put on the table! Thanks to Teresa, Brian, and David for believing in me and always blessing me with their "anything goes" attitude! Our son-in-law, Dave, and daughter-in-law, Stephanie, have added so much love and joy (and good genes!) to our family table and have so willingly joined in on our love of feasts and celebrations.

Thank you to my granddaughter, and kitchen buddy, Taylor Kay, for trying to like everything I cook! "I'm trying to like it, Grandma!" Thanks to Steven, my grandson, who really does like anything edible! And thanks to our little Allison, who already has that "Casey palate" and likes all kinds of food!

My mom and dad, Trula and Barry Casey, gave me this love for the kitchen. By raising us kids on delicious home cooking, Mother taught us what good food is all about. And Daddy's sheer joy and appreciation for food gave us that "Casey palate" that loves to taste, explore, and celebrate all food! They both taught me to see God's blessing in His creation of food, and in the fellowship good food brings.

My niece Julie Black is the backbone of our Food and Entertaining Cooking School here in Fort Worth. She manages our kitchens, where recipes are developed, tested, and taught. Her specialty is tying up loose ends and making things run smoothly.

Martha Stewart has been a huge inspiration to me, ever since I first took cooking lessons in her home and kitchens so many years ago. She validated my style of mixing and matching, collecting vintage dishes, and using my grandmother's linens. She has given new life and respect to this job of homemaking and has blazed the trail of teaching women to be their creative best in their homes.

Thanks to Kathy Peel, who got me started in books with our *Mother's Manual for Holiday Survival.* I will always appreciate her sharing projects with me and involving me in so many fun adventures. What an inspiration she is to women worldwide, to be smart and productive Family Managers.©

My book agent, Leslie Nunn, is one of the smartest and loveliest women I have ever met. Just having her represent me is a feather in my cap. What a gift when our friend Bill Hendricks gave me her name and said she might help me get my idea off the ground! She has done that and more, and I thank her for finding me my wonderful publisher, Promise Press.

My illustrator, John Schreiner, has created wonderful illustrations and made this book colorful and alive.

Promise Press has been wonderful in giving me freedom to write this book as I feel it can best help the everyday cook. Thank you to my editor, Susan Schlabach, for overseeing this project and making sure everything was done well. And thank you also to Kelly Kohl for all her work with the details of getting a book to press.

*Times* have changed. Family dinnertime is back! Parents have realized that there's just something about sitting down around the table and eating together that binds those family ties. But maybe you're an overbusy family manager who daily deals with tight schedules and double-parent burnout at the end of the day. The last thing you need is frustration over fixing dinner.

Or maybe you're like me. At the Peel house, we love to share meals with family, friends, and strangers. But there's just one slight problem. I'm not at my best in the kitchen (read: culinarily challenged).

Well, the book you're holding in your hands was written for you and me. Judie Byrd has come to our rescue. *Help! My Family's Hungry* includes easy instructions, helpful information, and wonderful menus that will get you out of the kitchen and around the table in record time!

Judie and I have been friends for almost twenty-five years. I've sat in her kitchen and watched her prepare countless delicious meals in minutes. My family has ribbed me: "Do you think you could learn to cook like Judie?" Now I can! And you can, too.

*Kathy Peel*
President, Family Manager, Inc.

# CHAPTER ONE
## Breakfast

## Survival Pantry

### DRY PANTRY:

Granola
Bananas
Apples
Bread
Oatmeal
Apple pie filling
Canned potatoes
Cinnamon
Honey
Maple flavoring

### REFRIGERATOR:

Eggs
Milk
Sausage
Bacon
Cream cheese

### FREEZER:

Several breakfast breads
Breakfast Cookies
Oatmeal muffins
Yogurt pops
Freezer strawberry jam
Grated cheddar cheese
New potatoes

# Breakfast

*If you're* like I was, just finding your way to the coffeepot is a feat on early school mornings. But breakfast can be a cozy and fun time with your kids, if you have a few tricks up your sleeve. In this chapter, I've included breakfast foods that helped make mornings easier for me when I was feeding three schoolkids.

There are several bread recipes included here because I found it was a lifesaver to keep loaves of interesting bread in the freezer. For breakfast, I sliced them, heated them a few minutes under the broiler, and served them with eggs, cold cereal, or alone with milk or hot chocolate. Kids think fruit breads are like dessert! With healthful ingredients like fruit, oats, and nuts, breads are nutritious as well as delicious.

Starting the day with breakfast together is the best way to send your kids out into the hectic world. But things do happen, and Breakfast Cookies and muffins are good for grabbing on the way out the door on those mornings when no one has time for anything more. Instead of letting a "bad morning" get you down, let your kids grab a nutritious cookie and glass of milk, and laugh it off in the car on the way to school.

# Breakfast Menu Ideas

## FIVE BUSY SCHOOL MORNINGS

1. Scrambled eggs with slices of Banana Bread
2. Granola with sliced fruit
3. Cinnamon toast with hot cereal
4. Morning Sunshine Smoothie with Breakfast Cookies
5. Toast and Freezer Strawberry Jam with Apple Raisin Oatmeal

## COZY SATURDAYS

Dad's Puffed Pancakes

## COMPANY BRUNCH

Sausage and Egg Casserole

## LAZY SATURDAY MORNING IN THE KITCHEN

Scrambled eggs, hash browns, bacon

## SLUMBER PARTY—THE MORNING AFTER!

Baked Stuffed French Toast

## FIVE MORE BUSY SCHOOL MORNINGS

1. Cheesy Scrambled Eggs with Oatmeal Muffins
2. Banana Whip with Breakfast Apple Cake
3. Strawberry Bread with Frozen Yogurt Pops
4. Fruit and Granola Parfaits with cinnamon toast
5. Toast with apple pie filling

# Morning Memories

*Your children,* when grown, will remember what went on in the mornings while they were growing up! Plan ahead to help breakfast time be nurturing and calm—a prelude to the hectic day ahead. It doesn't have to be every morning, but a great habit is to read just one or two Bible verses together at the start of the day. The night before, choose one verse from the Book of Proverbs. Since there are thirty-one chapters, you can go to the chapter that corresponds with the day of the month! Or look for a calendar that has a "verse of the day." This inspiration just might be the very thing your child needs for inner strength that day!

Following is a handy guide for having a quick morning Bible verse with your family. Remember to keep it fun! These verses might spark interesting conversation for your family.

---

### ONE-MONTH PROVERBS PLAN

| | | |
|---|---|---|
| Proverbs 1:8 | 12:15 | 23:15–16 |
| 2:6–7 | 13:14–16 | 24:1–2 |
| 3:3–4 | 14:26–27 | 25:11 |
| 4:5–6 or 23–26 | 15:1–2 | 26:12 |
| 5:21 | 16:3 | 27:17 |
| 6:6–8 | 17:17 | 28:6 |
| 7:1–4 | 18:10 | 29:7 |
| 8:11–13 | 19:20 | 30:25–28 |
| 9:10 | 20:11 | 31:8–9 |
| 10:27 | 21:21 | |
| 11:13–14 | 22:1 | |

## BANANA WHIP
Yield: 2 drinks

2 bananas
1 cup milk
1 tablespoon honey
1 teaspoon vanilla

- Place everything in a blender.
- Blend until smooth.
- Pour into 2 serving glasses.

## YOGURT ICY
Yield: 2 large drinks

1 cup plain or flavored yogurt
2 cups chopped fresh fruit
1 tablespoon honey or to taste
1 teaspoon vanilla
2 cups crushed ice

- Place yogurt, fruit, honey, and vanilla in a blender.
- Blend until smooth.
- Add ice and blend a few seconds.

## AMBROSIA SMOOTHIE
Yield: 3 drinks
*You can make up your own smoothies by using all kinds of fruit.*

1 cup milk
²⁄₃ cup orange
²⁄₃ cup pineapple juice
¹⁄₃ cup cream of coconut
1 banana
1 cup crushed ice

- Place all ingredients in a blender.
- Blend until smooth.

**Tip**

SOMETIMES THE GROCERY STORES WILL SELL DAY-OLD BANANAS FOR A SPECIAL PRICE. BUY THESE, PEEL THEM, AND WRAP EACH ONE IN PLASTIC WRAP. FREEZE THEM, AND THEN YOU ARE NEVER WITHOUT A BANANA FOR A QUICK SMOOTHIE. TO USE, MICROWAVE THE FROZEN BANANA FOR TEN SECONDS AND THEN PLACE IN THE BLENDER.

## IT'S THE BERRIES SMOOTHIE
Yield: 2 drinks

15 strawberries, fresh or frozen
$\frac{1}{2}$ cup raspberries, fresh or frozen
$\frac{1}{2}$ cup or more orange juice
1 tablespoon honey or 2 teaspoons sugar
1 teaspoon vanilla

• Place everything in a blender. If berries are frozen,
microwave them 10 seconds on high.
• Blend until smooth, adding more orange juice if desired.

## MORNING SUNSHINE SMOOTHIE
Yield: 2 drinks

2 bananas, peeled
$\frac{1}{2}$ cup strawberries or other berries, fresh or frozen
$\frac{1}{2}$ cup pineapple, fresh, frozen, or canned
1 cup orange juice or other fruit juice
1 teaspoon vanilla

• Place everything in a blender. If fruit is frozen,
microwave it for 10 seconds.
• Blend until smooth.
• Pour into 2 serving glasses.

*Save the juice from jars of maraschino cherries—it keeps indefinitely. Use it to flavor and color juices such as orange, pineapple, and grapefruit.*

## SPECIAL CHERRY ORANGE JUICE
Yield: about 1 quart

1-quart orange juice
$\frac{1}{2}$ cup maraschino cherry juice
Maraschino cherries

• Mix orange and cherry juices.
• Place cherries on toothpicks, 1 for each serving.
• Fill small glasses with ice and juice.
• Garnish with a cherry skewer.

## HOT BUTTERED APPLE CIDER MIX
Yield: 3 cups of mix

1 pound brown sugar
$\frac{1}{2}$ cup butter
1 teaspoon cinnamon
$\frac{1}{2}$ teaspoon ground cloves
$\frac{1}{4}$ teaspoon ground nutmeg

• Beat together all ingredients.
• Place in a bowl with a tight lid and refrigerate until needed.
(Can be refrigerated up to 6 weeks.)
• To make hot cider, place 1 heaping tablespoon of the mix in a cup
and fill with hot apple cider or juice.

*Keep a can of whipped cream (fat-free is delicious) in the refrigerator to top hot chocolate, breakfast breads, and hot cereal.*

## HOT CHOCOLATE MIX
Yield: 7 cups of dry mix

1 cup cocoa powder
$2\frac{1}{2}$ cups powdered sugar
2 cups dry, nondairy coffee creamer
2 cups nonfat dry milk powder

• Mix all ingredients together.
• Store in self-locking bags or container with tight-fitting lid.
• To make hot drink, place $\frac{1}{4}$ cup mix in a mug and fill with hot water.

## GRANOLA
Yield: 20 half-cup servings
*Granola can be kept frozen for up to 2 months.*
*Place in an airtight container or freezer bags.*

½ cup vegetable oil
½ cup honey
1 tablespoon cinnamon
5 cups uncooked old-fashioned oatmeal
1 cup sunflower seeds
½ cup sesame seeds
½ cup roasted soy nuts or papitas (pumpkin seeds)
½ cup wheat germ
½ cup wheat or oat bran
½ cup flaked coconut
½ cup chopped almonds or pecans
1 cup raisins

- Preheat oven to 325°. Spray a rimmed cookie sheet with vegetable oil.
- Combine vegetable oil, honey, and cinnamon in a small saucepan, heating mixture until the honey has melted.
- Combine the oatmeal, sunflower seeds, sesame seeds, soy nuts, wheat germ, wheat bran, coconut, and almonds in a large bowl.
- Pour honey mixture over dry ingredients, stirring until evenly coated.
- Spread granola on prepared pan. (Bake in batches if necessary.)
- Bake 20 to 25 minutes or until lightly browned, stirring mixture every 10 minutes.
- Remove from oven and stir in raisins.
- Store in an airtight container.

## FRUIT AND GRANOLA BREAKFAST PARFAITS
Yield: 2 servings

2 cups yogurt with fruit
1 cup of your favorite granola
1 cup grapes, sliced bananas, or sliced strawberries
Maraschino cherries

- Layer yogurt, granola, and fruit in parfait or stemmed glasses.
- Top with a maraschino cherry.

*Use a wire egg slicer to quickly slice strawberries, kiwi, or bananas into perfect slices.*

## APPLE RAISIN OATMEAL
### Yield: 4 servings

2 cups water
2 cups milk
2 cups regular rolled oats
1 teaspoon salt
2 apples, washed and cored but not peeled
½ cup raisins
1 teaspoon cinnamon
2 tablespoons sugar
1 tablespoon butter
Milk for serving
Brown sugar or maple syrup

- Place water, milk, oats, and salt in a saucepan; cover and bring to a boil over medium-high heat.
- Reduce heat to low and simmer 5 minutes.
- Use a grater to shred the apples; stir them, along with the raisins, into the oats.
- Stir together the cinnamon and sugar; then stir into the oats.
- Simmer until oats are tender, about another 5 minutes.
- Stir in the butter. Serve hot with milk and brown sugar.

YOU CAN SUBSTITUTE DATES OR OTHER DRIED FRUIT FOR THE RAISINS, AND PEARS OR PEACHES FOR THE APPLES.

## FRENCH TOAST
Yield: 4 large servings

4 eggs
¾ cup milk
¼ teaspoon salt
8 slices bread
2 tablespoons butter
Powdered sugar or cinnamon sugar
    for dusting

• In a large bowl, beat together the eggs,
    milk, and salt.
• Dip the bread slices into the mixture, turning
    to thoroughly coat both sides.
• Spray a nonstick skillet or griddle with vegetable
    oil, and then melt 1 tablespoon butter evenly in
    the bottom of the pan.
• Add half the bread slices and cook until golden brown on
    each side, turning once.
• Remove cooked bread. Melt more butter and cook the remaining bread
    in the same way.
• Dust with powdered sugar or cinnamon sugar and serve with maple syrup (page 19).

## CINNAMON AND SUGAR

Keep an interesting shaker filled with a mixture of cinnamon and sugar. This makes it easy for the kids to make their own cinnamon toast. This mixture also makes plain French toast a special treat. Just sprinkle on before pouring the syrup. A good mix is ½ cup sugar combined with 1 teaspoon cinnamon.

## BAKED STUFFED FRENCH TOAST
### Yield: 8 servings

8 thick slices French bread, crusts removed
1 package (8 ounces) cream cheese
½ cup golden raisins
½ cup chopped pecans
12 eggs
2 cups milk
⅓ cup maple syrup
2 tablespoons sugar
2 teaspoons cinnamon

- Spray a 9 x 13-inch baking dish with vegetable oil.
- Cut bread into small cubes and place ½ in bottom of baking dish.
- Cut cream cheese into small cubes and sprinkle over bread.
- Sprinkle on raisins and pecans.
- Top with remaining bread cubes.
- Beat together the eggs, milk, and maple syrup; pour over the bread.
- Stir together the sugar and cinnamon, and sprinkle over the egg and bread mixture.
- Let sit in refrigerator overnight.
- Preheat oven to 375°.
- Bake French toast 25 to 30 minutes or until golden brown.
- Serve with maple syrup.

### HOMEMADE MAPLE SYRUP

*Make your own maple syrup and serve it hot in a cute pitcher. Place 2 cups sugar and 1 cup water in a saucepan and bring to a simmer. Remove from the heat and stir in 1 teaspoon maple flavoring and 1 teaspoon vanilla. Stir until all sugar is dissolved.*

### DAD'S PUFFED PANCAKES
#### Yield: 4 to 6 servings

| Baking pan size | Butter | Eggs | Milk and flour |
| --- | --- | --- | --- |
| 2–3 quarts | ¼ cup | 3 | ¾ cup each |
| 3–4 quarts | ⅓ cup | 4 | 1 cup each |
| 4–4½ quarts | ½ cup | 5 | 1¼ cups each |
| 4½–5 quarts | ½ cup | 6 | 1½ cups each |

- Preheat oven to 425°.
- Place butter in baking pan and place in preheated oven.
- Meanwhile, place eggs in blender and whip on high speed for 1 minute.
- Add milk and turn on blender.
- With blender running, add the flour and continue blending for 30 seconds to mix well.
- Pour batter into the hot pan with melted butter.
- Return pan immediately to hot oven.
- Bake until puffy and golden brown, 20 to 25 minutes.
- Remove puffed pancake from oven and place on serving platter.
- Serve with maple syrup, jam, or powdered sugar and lemon juice.

*This is a great treat for dads to fix on Saturday mornings. My sister-in-law is raising three boys, and her husband serves this every Saturday morning to give Mom a break! The older boys now help Dad whip up these pancakes. What a great way for these boys to learn how dads can show love and care for their families. These waffles take a little planning, but they are well worth the effort. Stir these on Friday night for a special Saturday morning treat.*

## BACON AND CHEESE
## BREAKFAST PIZZAS
### Yield: 4 servings

*The mayonnaise in this recipe is a great addition, so give it a try!*
*For a low-fat version, try using low-fat mayonnaise, and turkey bacon, as well.*

4 slices bread
8 pieces bacon, cooked until crisp and then crumbled
12 thin slices tomato
Salt and pepper to taste
¼ cup mayonnaise
1 cup grated cheddar cheese

• Preheat broiler.
• Place bread on a baking sheet. Top each slice with 1 piece of the crumbled bacon, then tomato slices.
• Spread 1 tablespoon mayonnaise on top of tomatoes and top with cheese.
• Place baking sheet 4 inches from preheated broiler, and cook until hot and bubbly.

## CHEESY GRITS CASSEROLE
### Yield: 8 servings

*In the South, this is a popular dish to serve at Christmas breakfast. We like it for special breakfasts all year. Sometimes we stir in a small can of chopped green chilies and serve it with grilled steaks for dinner!*

*For easy morning cooking, assemble the whole casserole the night before, cover with plastic wrap, and refrigerate. Bake it the next morning.*

1 cup uncooked grits
4 cups water
½ cup butter
1 teaspoon salt
6-ounce package garlic cheese spread
2 eggs, beaten
¼ cup milk

• Preheat oven to 350°. Spray a two-quart baking dish with vegetable oil.
• Cook grits in water according to package directions.
• Stir remaining ingredients into cooked grits.
• Pour into prepared baking dish.
• Bake 45 minutes.

## BAKE THAT BACON

*Bacon is a great accompaniment for scrambled eggs. To make bacon for a large group, bake it in the oven. Preheat the oven to 350°. Lay the raw bacon pieces close together on a large baking sheet. Bake for 8 to 12 minutes or until done, turning once. Drain on paper towels.*

## CHEESY SCRAMBLED EGGS
### Yield: 2 servings

*Scrambled eggs are wonderful when you need to serve eggs to a crowd. Allow 2 eggs per serving and ½ cup cheese for each 4 eggs used.*

4 eggs
2 tablespoons milk
1 teaspoon salt
¼ teaspoon pepper
½ cup grated cheese, such as cheddar, Monterey Jack, or Swiss

• Beat together all ingredients.
• Heat a buttered skillet over medium-low heat and pour in the eggs.
• Stir with a wooden spatula, lifting the edges to let uncooked egg spread underneath.
• Cook eggs until they are almost set but still creamy.
• Remove to plates and serve immediately.

## SAUSAGE AND EGG CASSEROLE
### Yield: 6 to 8 servings

1 pound bulk sausage
8 slices sourdough French bread
4 cups grated cheddar cheese
6 eggs
3 cups milk
1 can (4 ounces) chopped green chilies
1 teaspoon salt
½ teaspoon pepper

• Place sausage in a skillet and fry quickly, chopping as it cooks until all pink is gone; drain on paper towels.
• Place the bread slices in the bottom of a 9 x 13-inch baking dish.
• Arrange the cooked sausage over the bread and top with the grated cheese.
• Beat the eggs, milk, green chilies, salt, and pepper together and pour over the sausage layer, saturating all the bread.
• Cover and refrigerate overnight.
• To serve, preheat oven to 320°, uncover casserole, and bake 1½ hours.

*Make up a breakfast casserole and then refrigerate it. Cut out individual servings and heat them quickly in the microwave. This makes 1 casserole last several days.*

LOSE THE FAT!

THIS CASSEROLE EASILY BECOMES LOW-FAT BY USING TURKEY SAUSAGE, REDUCED-FAT CHEDDAR CHEESE, SKIM MILK, AND LOW-FAT EGG PRODUCT.
IF YOU WANT TO SERVE THIS FOR DINNER, PUT IT ALL TOGETHER IN THE MORNING AND LEAVE IN THE REFRIGERATOR ALL DAY. BAKE AS DIRECTED.
IT ALSO FREEZES WELL. CONSTRUCT THE CASSEROLE AND COVER WITH PLASTIC WRAP AND THEN FOIL BEFORE PLACING IN THE FREEZER. BEFORE BAKING, ALLOW TO DEFROST OVERNIGHT IN THE REFRIGERATOR. BAKE AS DIRECTED.

## BREAKFAST COOKIES
### Yield: 1 dozen

1 cup butter, at room temperature
1 cup sugar
1 cup brown sugar
2 eggs
1 teaspoon vanilla
2 cups flour
1 teaspoon baking soda
1 teaspoon baking powder
½ teaspoon salt
2 cups instant rolled oats
1 cup Grape Nuts cereal
1 cup shredded coconut
½ cup raisins
½ cup chopped pecans or other nuts

- Preheat oven to 350°. Spray cookie sheets
  with vegetable oil.
- Beat together butter and sugars until fluffy.
- Add eggs and beat again. Scrape down sides of bowl.
- Stir together the flour, baking soda, baking powder, and salt.
  Stir into the butter mixture.
- Stir remaining ingredients into the batter.
- Drop by big spoonfuls onto prepared baking pans.
- Bake 10 to 12 minutes or until golden brown around the edges.

*Store these cookies in the freezer and pull out as needed.*
*Put servings on small plates (paper is okay!) the night before,*
*wrap with plastic wrap, and place on the breakfast table.*
*The next morning all you need to do is pour a glass of juice or milk.*
*If you don't get this far the night before, and they are frozen*
*in the morning, zap them 10 seconds in the microwave.*
*They are great served with hot chocolate in the winter*
*and cold milk in the summer!*

## ALMOND PUFF COFFEE CAKE
### Yield: 4 servings

1 cup water
½ cup butter
1 cup flour
4 eggs
1 tablespoon almond flavoring

- Preheat oven to 400°.
- In a large saucepan, bring the water and butter to a boil.
- While still on the heat, add flour all at once and beat until smooth.
- Remove from heat and add eggs, one at a time, beating well between each addition. Stir in almond flavoring.
- Scoop mixture onto an ungreased baking sheet, forming a smooth rectangle about 2 inches wide.
- Bake 20 minutes or until puffed and golden brown.
- Remove from oven and drizzle with Almond Glaze (recipe below).

## ALMOND GLAZE

2 cups powdered sugar
2 tablespoons milk
1 teaspoon almond flavoring
¼ cup sliced almonds

- Combine powdered sugar, milk, and almond flavoring. Beat well.
- Drizzle over baked coffee cake, and sprinkle on the almonds.

*Puff Magic*

*The batter for this coffee cake is the same as for making cream puffs.*
*To make individual little coffee cakes, plop spoonfuls of batter onto the baking sheet and spread lightly into circles. Bake 15 minutes or until just golden brown and dry.*

KOLACHES ARE SWEET, FLAKY POLISH PASTRIES FILLED WITH FRUIT, POPPY SEEDS, OR CREAM CHEESE. THEY USUALLY TAKE A LONG TIME TO MAKE, BUT THESE ARE SO QUICK AND EASY! THE "PASTRY FILL-ING" USED IN THESE IS DIFFERENT FROM PIE FILLING. IT IS MUCH STRONGER IN FLAVOR AND COMES IN A SMALLER CAN. THE BRAND I FIND IN MY GROCERY STORE IS CALLED *SOLO*. THESE KOLACHES ARE BEST EATEN WARM, AS SOON AS THEY ARE BAKED.

## EASY OPEN-FACE KOLACHES
### Yield: 40 pastries

2 cans (10 ounces each) refrigerated flaky biscuits
½ cup butter, melted
1 can (12 ounces) pastry filling such as apricot or cherry
4 tablespoons butter
6 tablespoons flour
½ cup sugar

- Preheat oven to 375°.
- Open cans of biscuits and separate each biscuit in half, making 40 pieces.
- Dip one side of each biscuit piece into the melted butter, and place buttered side up on an ungreased baking sheet.
- Make a large, deep thumbprint in the center of each biscuit.
- Place 1 teaspoon pastry filling in each thumbprint.
- Place the butter, flour, and sugar in a bowl.
  Use a fork to mix well until crumbly.
- Sprinkle this evenly over all 40 biscuits.
- Bake 15 to 20 minutes or until golden brown.

## CINNAMON SWIRL COFFEE CAKE
### Yield: 1 Bundt-sized coffee cake

1 package yellow cake mix
1 package (3 ounces) vanilla instant pudding
½ cup vegetable oil
4 eggs
1 cup sour cream
1 cup chopped pecans
¾ cup sugar
3 tablespoons cinnamon

- Preheat oven to 350°. Spray a Bundt pan
  with vegetable oil.
- Place cake mix, pudding mix, oil, eggs, and sour
  cream in a mixer bowl and beat on low with an
  electric mixer 8 minutes.
- In a small bowl, stir together remaining ingredients.
- Pour a third of the cake batter into prepared Bundt pan.
  Sprinkle ⅓ of the sugar mixture on top. Draw a knife through the two mixtures to
  create a marbled effect. Repeat this two more times, using remaining batter and
  sugar mixture.
- Bake for 1 hour. Cool in pan for 10 minutes and then dump out onto serving platter.

*My sister in California gave me this recipe when I was a newlywed.
It has been an old standby ever since. It makes a large cake that feeds
a crowd, and everyone always loves it. It is a great thing to take
to someone who is sick or just needs a little love from your kitchen!
Any leftover cake is wonderful sliced and toasted
in a skillet for breakfast!*

## RAISIN BRAN MUFFINS
### Yield: 6 dozen

*Good additions to these muffins would be ½ cup chopped pecans or raisins.
You could also stir in 1 teaspoon grated orange zest.*

6½ cups raisin bran cereal
5 cups flour
3 cups sugar
2 teaspoons salt
1 tablespoon baking soda
1-quart buttermilk

- Preheat oven to 375°. Line muffin tins with paper liners or spray with vegetable oil.
- Beat together all ingredients.
- Fill muffin tins ⅔ full and bake 20 minutes.

*This batter can be stored, tightly covered, in the refrigerator for up to 2 months! To use, fill the amount of muffin tins you need, and return batter to refrigerator.*

## OATMEAL MUFFINS
### Yield: 1 dozen

1 cup quick cooking oats
1 cup sour milk
1 egg
½ cup brown sugar
½ cup butter, melted
1 cup flour
1 teaspoon baking powder
½ teaspoon salt
½ teaspoon baking soda

- Preheat oven to 400°. Line muffin tins with paper liners or spray with vegetable oil.
- In a mixing bowl, soak oatmeal in sour milk for a few minutes until soft.
- Beat in the egg, sugar, and melted butter.
- Stir together the flour, baking powder, salt, and baking soda. Stir this carefully into the wet mixture. Stir just until dry ingredients are wet, taking care not to overstir (this causes muffins to be tough).
- Fill muffin tins ⅔ full and bake 15 to 20 minutes or until golden brown.

## GOOEY CINNAMON PULL-APART BREAD
### Yield: 12 to 16 servings

3 cans (10 ounces each) flaky refrigerated biscuits
   (such as Hungry Jack)
2 sticks butter
1½ cups brown sugar
1 tablespoon cinnamon
1 cup chopped pecans

- Preheat oven to 300°.
- Remove biscuits from cans and cut into quarters. *Cutting
  the biscuits into quarters is easy if you take a third of the roll
  at a time, lay it on its side, use a serrated knife to slice first
  in half, and then slice each half in half.*
- In a saucepan, heat butter, brown sugar, and cinnamon
  until butter is melted.
- Place half the biscuits in the bottom of a tube pan or
  Bundt pan.
- Top with half the melted butter mixture.
- Repeat layers.
- Bake 45 minutes.
- Remove from oven and let sit 5 minutes before turning
  onto a serving plate.

ONE SECRET OF HAVING A VERY MOIST AND SOFT BREAD IS TO NOT OVERBAKE. BE SURE TO TAKE THIS BREAD OUT OF THE OVEN AFTER JUST 45 MINUTES!

## FRESH APPLE PECAN BREAD
### Yield: 1 loaf
*The cheddar cheese gives this bread a moist texture and a wonderful flavor.*

½ cup butter
⅓ cup sugar
⅓ cup brown sugar
2 eggs
½ cup grated cheddar cheese
2 cups flour
1 teaspoon baking powder
½ teaspoon baking soda
½ teaspoon salt
1½ cups shredded apples
1 cup chopped pecans

- Preheat oven to 350°. Spray a loaf pan with vegetable oil.
- Beat together the butter and sugars until fluffy.
- Add eggs and beat again. Scrape down the sides of the bowl.
- Stir in the cheddar cheese.
- Stir together the flour, baking powder, soda, and salt. Stir into the butter mixture.
- Stir in the apples and chopped pecans.

## GRANDMA CASEY'S BANANA BREAD
### Yield: 1 loaf

1 cup sugar
1 stick butter
2 eggs
3 ripe bananas, mashed
1¾ cups flour
¼ teaspoon salt
1 teaspoon baking soda
½ teaspoon baking powder

- Preheat oven to 350°. Grease and flour a loaf pan.
- Mix all ingredients together with a mixer just until combined well.
- Pour in prepared loaf pan, and bake 40 minutes or until a toothpick comes out clean from the center.

## STRAWBERRY BREAD
### Yield: 2 loaves

4 eggs
2 cups sugar
2 cups frozen strawberries, thawed
1¼ cups vegetable oil
3 cups flour
1 teaspoon baking soda
1 teaspoon salt
1 tablespoon cinnamon
1 cup chopped pecans or other nuts

- Preheat oven to 350°. Spray a loaf pan with vegetable oil.
- Beat together the eggs, sugar, strawberries, and vegetable oil.
- Stir together the flour, baking soda, salt, and cinnamon. Stir into the egg mixture.
- Stir in the pecans.
- Pour batter into the prepared loaf pan.
- Bake 1 hour or until toothpick inserted into the center comes out clean.
- Remove from the oven and allow to sit 5 minutes before removing from the pan. To help the loaf come out easily, run a sharp knife along the outside of the loaf, separating it from the pan.

*My friend Carol is one of those people who magically seems to be able to produce something fabulous to eat at a moment's notice. Once she called me over for a quick cup of coffee. As I walked in her kitchen, she was pulling a loaf of this bread out of her oven. What a gift it is to treat a friend to a cup of coffee and a slice of hot, homemade strawberry bread!*

*Keep a loaf of this in your freezer. Put the loaf out on the counter before going to bed, and the next morning you can treat your family to a big, thick slice!*

## BREAKFAST APPLE CAKE
### Yield: 1 Bundt cake
*This cake is very moist and will keep 2 weeks in the refrigerator if wrapped well.*

1 can apple pie filling
2 cups sugar
½ cup vegetable oil
1 teaspoon vanilla
2 eggs
2 cups flour
1 teaspoon salt
1 teaspoon cinnamon
2 teaspoons baking soda
1 cup chopped pecans

*When testing a Bundt cake for doneness, a toothpick might not be long enough. Use a strand of uncooked spaghetti instead.*

- Preheat oven to 325°. Spray a Bundt pan with vegetable oil.
- In a large bowl, combine apple pie filling, sugar, vegetable oil, vanilla, and eggs; beat well with a spoon.
- Combine dry ingredients and stir into apple mixture.
- Pour into prepared Bundt pan.
- Bake 55 to 60 minutes or until a toothpick comes out clean from the center.
- Allow to cool in pan for 15 minutes and then invert onto serving plate.
- Serve with Maple Butter (recipe below) or whipped cream, if desired.

## MAPLE BUTTER

1 stick butter
¼ cup maple syrup
1 tablespoon powdered sugar

- Beat all together until well blended.
- Cover and store in the refrigerator up to 2 months.

## CARROT BREAD
### Yield: 1 loaf

1 cup sugar
¾ cup oil
2 eggs
1½ cups flour
1 teaspoon baking powder
1 teaspoon baking soda
1 teaspoon cinnamon
¼ teaspoon salt
1 cup grated carrots

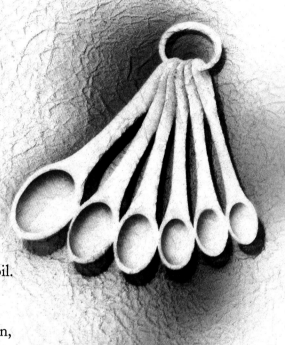

- Preheat oven to 350°. Lightly spray a
  loaf pan with oil and dust lightly
  with flour.
- In a mixer bowl, cream the sugar and oil.
- Beat in the eggs.
- In a small bowl, stir together the flour,
  baking powder, baking soda, cinnamon,
  and salt.
- Stir flour mixture into creamed mixture,
  and then stir in the carrots.
- Pack into prepared loaf pan.
- Bake 35 minutes or until toothpick comes out clean from the center.

TO SERVE FREEZER JAMS, LET SIT AT ROOM TEMPERATURE A FEW MINUTES UNTIL JUST SOFT ENOUGH TO SPOON OUT OF THE JAR. RETURN UNUSED PORTION TO THE FREEZER. THESE FREEZER JAMS ARE DELICIOUS SERVED ON HOT WAFFLES, PANCAKES, OR TOAST.

*Store in freezer for up to 6 months or refrigerate for up to 3 weeks.*

## UNCOOKED PEACH JAM
### Yield: about 5½ cups

2 cups peeled peaches, fresh or frozen
4 cups sugar
1 cup water
1 package powdered pectin

- Place peaches in blender, and blend until mashed.
- Add sugar, and blend until well mixed.
- Allow mixture to stand for 30 minutes, blending a few seconds occasionally to dissolve the sugar.
- Place water in a saucepan and stir in the pectin.
- Bring to a boil and boil rapidly 1 minute, stirring constantly.
- Remove from heat and add peaches. Stir for 2 minutes.
- Pour into clean jelly glasses, leaving ½-inch space at top.
- Cover with lids and let stand at room temperature until set, about 24 hours.

## FREEZER STRAWBERRY JAM
### Yield: about 4 cups

1¾ cups strawberries, trimmed and crushed
4 cups sugar
2 tablespoons fresh lemon juice
1 pouch liquid fruit pectin

- Place fruit in a large, nonaluminum bowl; add sugar and stir well.
- Allow to sit for 10 minutes, stirring occasionally.
- Add lemon juice and fruit pectin. Stir to dissolve.
- Pour into clean jelly glasses, leaving ½-inch space at top.
- Cover with lids and let stand at room temperature until cool.

CHAPTER TWO

*Lunch*

# Lunchtime

Some of my best childhood memories are the summers my family spent at our little cabin up in Oak Creek Canyon, Arizona. My dad would go home and work during the week, then come up and join us each weekend. We were right on the creek, and we ate fried rainbow trout for dinner almost every night—all crispy and salty with cornmeal. Mother said we needed to eat up the fish, so she and my brother could catch more the next day.

Lunches were the best part of the day. Mother would peel and thickly slice ripe, juicy tomatoes. She would make Thousand Island dressing to put on top, and we'd eat platefuls. We'd all help make tuna, egg salad, or chicken sandwiches on wonderful soft, white bread with Mother's homemade mayonnaise. And we'd have macaroni salad, the kind with lots of good things chopped into it like bell pepper, pimentos, and onions. After lunch, the daily afternoon rain showers would move in, and we'd take naps on the screened-in porch.

Look for opportunities to make unique memories for your family. Saturday lunches can be loads of fun, and impromptu picnics are a great occasion for starting family traditions—use a favorite quilt, topped with vintage aprons as place mats. Collect plastic cups with funny logos; and use bright napkins, paper plates, and cutlery. Surprise each person with his favorite candy bar for dessert.

## Dessert ideas:

Trail mix
Assorted nuts and raisins
Applesauce
Pudding
Cookies
Pound cake slices

## Side item ideas:

Bell pepper, carrot, cucumber, celery
Pickles, olives
Deviled eggs
Chips
Oyster crackers
Sliced apples (drizzle with lemon juice)
Cheese sticks or slices

## Sandwich filling ideas:

Sliced meats: turkey, ham, beef, chicken,
    pastrami, salami
Thinly sliced meat loaf with ketchup
Chicken salad with chopped apples
    and/or raisins
Bacon with tomato slices and lettuce
Sliced or grated cheese: cheddar, Swiss,
    mozzarella
Pimento cheese
Cream cheese with pineapple
Cream cheese with chopped, sun-dried
    tomatoes and basil
Egg, tuna, or chicken salad

## Survival Pantry

DRY PANTRY:
Bread: French loaf, English
    muffins, sandwich bread
Canned tuna
Bottled pimentos
Pickle relish
Mayonnaise
Mustard
Crackers and chips
Bottled salsa
Tomato juice
Salad dressings
Canned soup: vegetable,
    tomato
Canned beans: ranch-style
    black beans
Cookies

REFRIGERATOR:
Fresh fruit
Sandwich meats
Eggs
Lemons
Melons
Cabbage
Salad vegetables and lettuce
Cheese
Prepared tortellini
Tortillas

FREEZER:
Corn and peas

# Lunch Menus

### SPRING-CLEANING SATURDAYS

1. The Big Sub Sandwich with fresh fruit salad
2. Egg or Tuna Salad Sandwiches with Homemade Bread and Butter Pickles and chips
3. Slivered Iceberg and Tuna Salad with saltine crackers

### THE DOG-DAYS-OF-SUMMER SATURDAYS

1. Greek Salad with an assortment of crackers
2. Gazpacho with chips and salsa
3. Smoked Turkey and Peach Salad with crusty sourdough bread

### BLUSTERY FALL SATURDAYS

1. My Mom's Potato Soup with toasted cheese sandwiches
2. Hot Stuffed Cheese Rolls with Sweet Marinated Slaw

### COZY WINTER SATURDAYS

1. Toasted Pimento Cheese Sandwiches with tomato soup and potato chips
2. Warm Tortellini Salad with slices of country-style bread

### GET PACKIN'-SCHOOL LUNCH IDEAS

1. Club Sandwiches, melon slices, chips, and cookies
2. Corn and Black Bean Salad with corn chips and sliced Vanilla Wafer Cake

## BERRY JUICY PUNCH
Yield: about 1 quart

1 can (6 ounces) frozen mixed berry juice
1 can (6 ounces) frozen grape juice
1 can (6 ounces) frozen lemonade

• In a 2-quart container, prepare each can of juice
according to directions on can.
• Stir to dissolve well and serve.

---

## FRUITY ICE CUBES

*For a special treat, make ice cubes that are tasty and won't water down your drinks! Buy old-fashioned ice cube trays and use them to make ice cubes, using fruit-flavored Koolaid or Tang. When your drink is gone, you still have the ice cubes to crunch on!*

## MINT TEA
Yield: approximately 1 gallon

3 cups sugar
1½ cups bottled lemon juice
8 tea bags
½ cup mint leaves

• Place sugar and lemon juice in a saucepan and bring to a simmer,
stirring to dissolve sugar.
• Turn off heat. Add 8 tea bags and mint leaves.
• Cover and steep for 20 minutes. Strain mixture.
• Add water to make 1 gallon.

---

## SPICED ALMOND TEA
Yield: 3 quarts

3 quarts water
1¼ cups sugar
3 tablespoons instant tea mix
1 can (12 ounces) frozen lemonade, undiluted
1 tablespoon almond extract
1 tablespoon vanilla

• Combine all ingredients and stir until sugar is dissolved.

A TASTY
LITTLE TRICK
IS TO PLACE A
SLICE OF CHEESE
(OR A LITTLE
GRATED CHEESE)
IN THE BOTTOM
OF THE SOUP
BOWL BEFORE
YOU LADLE IN
THE HOT SOUP.
MMM—A HOT,
MELTED SURPRISE
FOR CHEESE
LOVERS!

## VEGETABLE CHOWDER
### Yield: 6 servings

4 slices bacon, cut into slivers
1½ cups chopped onions
1 green bell pepper, chopped
3 cups frozen mixed vegetables
3 cups milk
2 teaspoons salt
¼ teaspoon pepper
2 tablespoons chopped pimentos

• In a Dutch oven, fry bacon slivers until almost crisp.
• Add onions and peppers and cook until tender.
• Add corn; cover and simmer 10 minutes.
• Remove lid and break up any frozen pieces of corn.
• Simmer 5 minutes uncovered or until all corn is cooked.
• Add milk, salt, and pepper. Simmer 5 minutes.
• Stir in pimentos and serve.

*For a fun treat:*

Serve Vegetable Chowder in bread bowls. Divide 1 loaf of prepared frozen bread dough (available in the frozen food section of the grocery store) into fourths. Place each piece in each of 4 greased muffin tins (place far enough apart that each has room to rise and spread). Allow to rise until doubled. Bake in preheated, 375° oven for 12 minutes or until golden brown. Allow to cool, and then use a serrated knife to carve out the centers to form bowls. Be sure to leave a thick layer at the bottom. Fill with soup and serve immediately. As you eat the soup, pinch off pieces of bread.

## EASY FRENCH ONION SOUP
### Yield: 6 servings
*Serve this soup with a dinner salad, fruit salad, or with a sandwich.*

¼ cup olive oil or vegetable oil
2 large onions, peeled and thinly sliced
6 cups beef stock
Salt and pepper to taste
Parmesan Toast (recipe below)

• Heat olive oil in a large soup pot over medium-high heat.
• Add onions and cook for 15 to 20 minutes, stirring occasionally until golden brown and caramelized.
• Add beef stock. Cover and simmer another 20 minutes.
• Add salt and pepper.
• Ladle into soup bowls or mugs and top with Parmesan Toast.

## PARMESAN TOAST

• Butter slices of French bread and sprinkle each with Parmesan cheese.
• Place under broiler and cook until golden brown.
• Store in zip-fastened bags up to 3 days at room temperature or 1 month in the freezer.

## MY MOM'S POTATO SOUP
### Yield: about 1 serving for each big spoonful of mashed potatoes
*This soup goes well with additions such as cheddar cheese (stir it in at the last, and heat just long enough for the cheese to melt), chopped ham, pimentos, corn, peas, or other vegetables.*

Leftover mashed potatoes
Enough milk to make consistency of thick soup
Salt and pepper to taste

• Place mashed potatoes in a large saucepan.
• Add milk and use a potato masher or whisk to chop up potatoes.
• Heat just to a simmer.
• Add salt and pepper to taste.
• Serve piping hot!

PREPARED FROZEN
ONIONS AND
PEPPERS
SAVE TIME.
USE DIRECTLY
FROM THE FREEZER
BAG, AND THEN
RESEAL THE BAG
WITH A TWIST TIE
AND RETURN TO
THE FREEZER.

## BEEF TACO SOUP
Yield: 8 to 10 servings

1 pound ground beef
1 cup chopped onion
1 bell pepper, chopped
1 can (28 ounces) chopped tomatoes with juice
1½ cups frozen corn
2 cans (15 ounces each) pinto beans
1 package dry ranch dressing mix
1 package dry taco seasoning
Corn chips

• Brown ground beef with onion and pepper.
• Add remaining ingredients and simmer for 20 minutes.
• To serve, sprinkle crushed corn chips on top.

## HEARTY RANCH BEAN SOUP
Yield: 8 to 10 servings

1 pound ground beef
1 onion, chopped
1 jar (26 ounces) prepared spaghetti sauce
1 cup chicken stock
2 cans (10 ounces each) spicy tomatoes with chilies
1 can (15 ounces) ranch-style beans

• In a large soup pot, brown meat with onion; drain off fat.
• Add remaining ingredients.
• Cover and simmer 35 minutes.

# ITALIAN SPINACH AND RICE SOUP
### Yield: 6 servings

2 tablespoons olive oil
2 cups chopped onions
1 medium bell pepper, chopped
6 cups chicken broth
½ cup uncooked rice
2 packages (10 ounces each) frozen,
    chopped spinach
Salt and pepper to taste
Parmesan cheese for serving

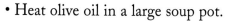

• Heat olive oil in a large soup pot.
• Sauté onions and pepper until tender.
• Add broth and rice; cover and simmer 10 minutes.
• Add spinach and simmer another 10 minutes or until
    rice is tender and spinach is cooked.
• Add salt and pepper.
• Ladle into soup bowls and top with Parmesan cheese.

*This soup can easily become Italian Spinach and Tortellini Soup:*
*Omit the rice. Add prepared tortellini to soup along with the spinach.*
*If the tortellini is dried, you might need to add a few minutes*
*of cooking time to thoroughly cook the pasta.*
*Serve this soup with slices of Garlicky Toast.*

## GAZPACHO
### Yield: 4 to 6 servings
*This soup is great served with chips and taco dip
or guacamole.*

2 tomatoes or 1 can (15 ounces) tomatoes with juice
½ green bell pepper
1 rib celery
¼ small onion
1 cucumber, peeled
Several sprigs of cilantro or parsley
1 can (4 ounces) diced green chilies
½ teaspoon minced fresh garlic or ½ teaspoon garlic salt
1 cup tomato juice
1 tablespoon olive oil
1 tablespoon vinegar (cider, white, wine, rice, or
    whatever you have)
Salt and pepper to taste

GAZPACHO. . .
*is a Spanish
soup and is generally
served cold.
You can, however,
serve it heated
in mugs.*

- Lightly chop all vegetables and place in blender.
- Add remaining ingredients, and blend or pulse numerous times until of desired consistency.
- Refrigerate until cold and serve chilled.

*The cilantro and green chilies in this recipe
are not essential
but give the soup a Southwestern flavor.*

## BAKED POTATO SOUP
### Yield: 6 to 8 servings
*Use leftover baked potatoes in this recipe.*
*You'll find yourself baking extras just to make this soup!*

LOW-FAT TIP:
*Use turkey bacon, or drain off all the fat and add 1 tablespoon vegetable oil.*
*Use low-fat cheddar cheese and sour cream.*

6 slices bacon, slivered*
1 cup chopped onion
⅔ cup flour
6 cups chicken broth
4 cups diced baked potatoes
2 cups milk
¼ cup chopped parsley
2 teaspoons garlic powder
2 teaspoons crushed basil
2 teaspoons salt
½ teaspoon pepper
Several drops Tabasco sauce
1 cup grated cheddar cheese
½ cup sliced green onions
Extra bacon and cheddar cheese for garnish
⅔ cup sour cream for garnish

- Place bacon and onion in a soup pot or large saucepan and cook until bacon is done. Drain off all but 2 tablespoons of the grease.
- Use a whisk to stir in the flour. Cook 2 to 3 minutes, stirring constantly.
- Add chicken stock gradually, whisking to prevent lumps. Cook and stir until mixture thickens.
- Add potatoes, milk, parsley, garlic powder, basil, salt, and pepper. Simmer 5 minutes.
- Stir in Tabasco sauce to taste.
- Add grated cheese and green onion, and stir until cheese melts.
- Ladle into soup bowls. If desired, top with more crisp bacon, grated cheese, and a dollop of sour cream.

*To easily sliver the bacon, hold the slices together on a cutting board and use a sharp knife to cut across the short ends, making thin slivers. To keep the pieces from sticking together while cooking, use a spatula to stir and break them apart.*

## MOM'S WORLD-FAMOUS VEGETABLE SOUP
### Yield: 6 to 8 servings

*To make this a meat soup, add chopped, cooked beef (leftover roast beef),*
*chicken, or ham along with the vegetables.*

1 can (28 ounces) chopped tomatoes with juice
4 cups water or chicken stock
1 large onion, chopped
2 medium carrots, sliced
3 ribs celery, sliced
1 small bell pepper, chopped
2 cups coarsely chopped cabbage
1 bay leaf
1 teaspoon each, dried basil and rosemary
Salt and pepper to taste
1 cup frozen corn
½ cup frozen peas

• Place the first 9 ingredients in a large soup pot.
• Cover and simmer gently for 30 to 40 minutes or until all vegetables are tender.
• Add remaining ingredients and cook until all soup is heated.

## CHICKEN STOCK

*Many recipes call for chicken stock.*
*You can use bouillon cubes, granules,*
*or chicken base. (Chicken base comes in*
*a container where you buy soups.*
*It doesn't need to be refrigerated;*
*just store it in the dry pantry.)*
*If you use these, follow the directions*
*on the labels. To save mixing,*
*just add the cubes, granules,*
*or base along with water straight*
*to the recipe and stir in.*

## SIMPLE HOMEMADE CHICKEN STOCK

This is a great place to use the carcass from a baked, roasted, or smoked chicken. Place it in a large soup pot and cover with water. Add one chopped onion, several chopped ribs of celery, 1 bay leaf, and 2 tablespoons chicken base. Simmer, uncovered, for 2 hours. Skim off fat. (To get every bit of fat off, refrigerate overnight and then skim off the fat that has risen to the top and become solid.)

## CHILI CON QUESO SOUP
### Yield: 8 servings

1 can (10½ ounces) cream of celery soup, undiluted
1 can (15 ounces) chopped tomatoes with chilies
1 cup frozen, chopped onions
1 can (4½ ounces) chopped green chilies
4 ounces processed cheese (Velveeta), cubed
1 cup grated cheddar cheese
2 cups small corn chips
1 cup sour cream

• In a saucepan, combine soup, tomatoes, onions, and chilies; heat to simmering.
• Stir in cheese and heat until melted and smooth.
• Spoon into soup bowls and top with cheddar cheese, corn chips, and a dollop of sour cream.

## QUICK AND EASY WILD RICE SOUP
### Yield: 6 to 8 cups

2 cans (15 ounces each) chicken broth
1 can (15 ounces) cream of potato soup
1 cup cooked wild rice
3 ribs celery, chopped
1 onion, chopped
3 carrots, chopped
1 can (4 ounces) sliced mushrooms
½ cup slivered almonds
1 cup grated cheddar cheese
2 cups half-and-half
6 slices bacon, cooked and crumbled

• Place first 8 ingredients in a soup pot and simmer gently 15 minutes.
• Stir in remaining ingredients, and heat just long enough to melt cheese and heat thoroughly.

## ZIPPED-UP VEGGIE SOUP
### Yield: 2 to 3 servings

1 can (15½ ounces) condensed vegetable soup
1 soup can of water
¼ cup frozen corn
¼ cup frozen peas

• Combine all ingredients in a small saucepan and heat to a simmer.

## PERFECT HARD-BOILED EGGS

• Place uncooked eggs in a saucepan and add water to cover. Place on high heat and cook until water just begins to boil. (Do *not* allow to boil!)

• Immediately cover the saucepan with a lid and remove from the heat. Allow the eggs to sit for 20 minutes. Then, pour off the water and let cold water run into the pan for a few minutes. Ta-da! Peel one and see! No green line and perfectly cooked yolks. The secret is to not let the water boil and the 20 minutes of gentle heat. You will be so proud of your hard-boiled eggs.

## EGG SALAD SANDWICH FILLING
Yield: about 1¼ cups,
enough for 4 to 5 sandwiches

4 hard-cooked eggs
¼ cup mayonnaise
2 teaspoons Dijon or yellow mustard, if desired
1 to 2 tablespoons pickle relish, dill or sweet (your choice)
1 tablespoon pickle juice from sweet or dill pickles or
1 tablespoon white or cider vinegar
½ teaspoon dried dill weed, if desired
Salt and pepper to taste

• Grate or chop eggs and place in a bowl.
• Add remaining ingredients and blend well.
• Add extra pickle relish or pickle juice as needed or desired.

## TUNA SALAD SANDWICH FILLING
Yield: about 3½ cups,
enough for 6 to 8 sandwiches

2 cans (6½ ounces each) tuna, drained
2 hard-cooked eggs, chopped or grated
½ cup pickle relish
½ to ¾ cup finely chopped celery
⅓ to ½ cup mayonnaise
1 tablespoon Dijon or yellow mustard, if desired
Salt and pepper to taste

• Blend together all ingredients.
• Check for enough salt and pepper, and add more mayonnaise if needed.

## PIMENTO CHEESE SANDWICH FILLING
Yield: about 1½ cups, enough for 4 to 6 sandwiches

3 cups finely grated cheddar cheese
1 tablespoon finely grated onion
⅓ cup finely chopped pimento
2 tablespoons Dijon mustard
⅓ to ½ cup mayonnaise

• Place all ingredients in mixer bowl or food processor and beat until well blended.
• Add extra mayonnaise and up to 1 tablespoon of milk if needed to obtain spreading consistency.

USE COOKIE CUTTERS TO CUT OUT THE BREAD WHEN YOU MAKE SANDWICHES FOR YOUR KIDS. ANY SANDWICH WILL BE MORE ATTRACTIVE AND INTERESTING WHEN CUT INTO A FUNNY SHAPE.

*Start a collection of cookie cutters. And while you're at it, start a collection for your children! When they are grown, it will be a valuable, useful collection they can use in their own kitchens.*

## HOMEMADE PEANUT BUTTER

2 cups roasted, shelled peanuts
2 teaspoons vegetable or peanut oil
½ teaspoon salt (omit if peanuts are salted)

• Place ingredients in a food processor and process until mixture is smooth and spreadable.
• Stop the machine every so often to scrape the sides.
• Store in a covered canning jar in the refrigerator.

## FRUITWICH

2 tablespoons cream cheese, softened
1 tablespoon chopped peanuts
½ apple, cored and thinly sliced
A few drops of lemon juice
2 slices raisin or banana bread

• Combine cream cheese and peanuts.
• Drizzle apples with lemon juice to keep them from browning.
• Layer cream cheese mixture and apples on 1 slice of bread.
• Top with remaining slice of bread.

## Sandwich Surprises!
*Interesting and unique sandwiches for fun lunches.*

### PB & BS

Raisin bread
Peanut butter
Crispy bacon, crumbled

- Lightly spread peanut butter on two slices of bread.
- Sprinkle some bacon on top of one slice of bread.
- Top with second slice of bread.

### PB AND BANANAS

Raisin bread
Peanut butter
Sliced bananas

- Make sandwiches using raisin bread, peanut butter,
and sliced bananas.

### APPLE-BANS

2 slices bread
2 teaspoons butter or mayonnaise
½ apple, peeled, cored, and thinly sliced
½ banana, sliced
1 teaspoon cinnamon and sugar mixture

- Spread butter or mayonnaise on bread.
- Layer sliced fruit on top of one slice of bread.
- Sprinkle with cinnamon and sugar mixture.
- Top with remaining slice of bread.

## CHICKEN SALAD FOR SANDWICHES
Yield: about 1½ cups,
enough for 3 to 4 sandwiches

2 chicken breast halves, cooked and chopped
2 ribs celery, finely chopped
¼ cup pickle relish
½ cup mayonnaise, or half sour cream, if desired
Salt and pepper to taste

• Combine all ingredients and mix well.

## HAWAIIAN CHICKEN SALAD
Stir in ½ cup well-drained pineapple tidbits and ¼ cup chopped macadamia nuts or pecans.

## TARRAGON CHICKEN SALAD FOR SANDWICHES
Yield: about 1½ cups,
enough for 3 to 4 sandwiches

2 chicken breast halves, cooked and chopped
3 ribs celery, finely chopped
½ cup sliced almonds
2 teaspoons dried, crushed tarragon
¼ cup mayonnaise
2 tablespoons sour cream
Salt and pepper to taste

• Combine all ingredients and mix well.

*Other additions
for Chicken Salad:*

½ cup finely
chopped apples
2 slices bacon, crisply
cooked and chopped
½ cup sliced grapes
¼ cup raisins
1 tablespoon small capers
2 tablespoons chopped,
green stuffed olives
½ cup grated
cheddar cheese

## BACON-DATE SUPREMES

2 slices wheat or raisin bread
2 teaspoons butter or mayonnaise
2 slices crispy bacon
3 or 4 chopped dates or 2 tablespoons raisins

• Spread butter or mayonnaise on bread.
• Layer bacon and dates (or raisins) on one slice of bread.
• Top with remaining slice of bread.

## GREEK CHICKEN PITAS
### Yield: 4 to 6 sandwiches

4 ounces feta cheese, crumbled
2 medium tomatoes, diced
1 cucumber, peeled and diced
1 small red onion, thinly sliced
¼ cup sliced black olives
1 cup chopped or sliced cooked chicken
3 tablespoons olive or vegetable oil
1 tablespoon lemon juice
1 teaspoon dried oregano
Salt and pepper to taste
Lettuce leaves
3 or 4 pita loaves, halved
Alfalfa sprouts

- Combine cheese, tomatoes,
  cucumber, onion, olives,
  and chicken.
- In a small bowl, whisk together
  the olive or vegetable oil, lemon juice,
  oregano, salt, and pepper. Toss with the salad mixture.
- Line each pita half with lettuce and fill with salad.
- Top with alfalfa sprouts and serve.

## THE BIG SUB SANDWICH
### Yield: 1 large sandwich to serve 4 to 6
*This sandwich appeared regularly at our house on Saturdays.
It is easy to whip together and serves lots.*

1 large loaf French bread, about 12 inches long
8 ounces sliced meats (ham, turkey, chicken, or roast beef)
½ onion, thinly sliced
2 tomatoes, thinly sliced
½ cup grated cheese, cheddar or other
Sliced green bell pepper
Shredded lettuce
¼ to ½ cup Italian salad dressing

• Slice bread lengthwise.
• Layer sandwich ingredients on bottom piece of bread.
• Drizzle with Italian salad dressing.
• Cut into serving pieces and serve from cutting board or
  large platter.

## CLUB SANDWICH

3 pieces bread (may be toasted)
2 tablespoons mayonnaise or other spread
2 ounces thinly sliced ham, turkey, chicken, or roast beef
3 thin slices tomato
2 lettuce leaves
Slice of cheddar or Swiss cheese
1 slice bacon, cooked crisp

• Spread mayonnaise on 1 slice of bread and top with
  sliced meat, tomatoes, and 1 lettuce leaf.
• Spread mayonnaise on another slice of bread and place
  on top.
• Layer on cheese, bacon, and remaining lettuce leaf.
• Spread mayonnaise on remaining slice of bread and
  place on top.
• Cut sandwich into halves on the diagonal.

### CLUB AND SUB PITAS

*Many sandwiches can be made using pita bread. Cut the round pieces of pita in half; open and stuff with ingredients.*

*Hearty sandwiches like these can be served with a bowl of soup for a quick meal during the busy workweek. Use whatever you have on hand for either sandwich.*

53

## REUBEN SANDWICH

1 tablespoon soft butter or vegetable oil
2 pieces rye bread
Slices of Swiss cheese to cover bread
1 tablespoon Thousand Island Dressing or mustard
¼ cup well-drained sauerkraut
2 to 3 ounces thinly sliced pastrami or corned beef

- Spread butter evenly on 1 side of each piece of bread.
- Heat a small skillet over medium heat and place 1 piece of bread, buttered side down, in heated skillet.
- Cover bread with Swiss cheese and then add the dressing or mustard.
- Layer with sauerkraut and pastrami. Top with second piece of bread, buttered side up.
- Cover with a plate or small saucepan lid and allow to cook for 2 to 3 minutes, or until bottom is lightly browned.
- Turn sandwich over and repeat for other side.

## MONTE CRISTO SANDWICH

4 tablespoons soft butter
3 slices bread
Thinly sliced turkey, chicken, or ham to cover bread
Sliced cheddar or Swiss cheese to cover bread
1 egg
¼ cup milk
⅛ teaspoon salt
2 tablespoons butter or vegetable oil for toasting
Maple syrup, if desired

- Butter 1 side of 2 slices of bread. Butter 2 sides of third slice of bread.
- Place turkey slices on 1 buttered slice.
- Top with doubly buttered slice.
- Place cheese on top and cover with remaining bread, buttered side down.
- In a flat soup bowl, beat together the egg, milk, and salt.
- Dip the sandwich into the egg mixture, coating edges and sides well.
- Heat 1 tablespoon butter in skillet over medium heat.
- Add dipped sandwich and cook 2 to 3 minutes, or until golden brown on the bottom.
- Turn sandwich and repeat, pressing lightly with a pancake turner or spatula.
- Serve with maple syrup, if desired.

THINK OF THIS HEARTY SANDWICH WHEN UNEXPECTED COMPANY ARRIVES. IT IS AN IMPRESSIVE ENTRÉE, AND MOST OF THE INGREDIENTS CAN BE KEPT ON HAND.

## Comfort Food!

*Make onion sandwiches for a quick supper or midnight snack.*

*Layer paper-thin onion slices and slices of cheddar cheese between slices of really good white or wheat bread. Use either mustard or mayonnaise, depending on your taste. Make these when sweet Vidalia or Mayan onions are available.*

## BAKED CRESCENT MELTS
### Yield: 4 servings

1 package (8 ounces) refrigerated crescent roll dough
4 teaspoons mayonnaise or mustard
Sliced ham, turkey, or chicken to cover rolls
Sliced or grated cheddar or Swiss cheese to cover rolls

• Preheat oven to 375°.
• Separate triangles of dough and press lightly into shape.
• Spread each with mayonnaise or mustard.
• Layer with meat and cheese.
• Starting with the wide end, roll up each piece of dough into a crescent shape.
• Place on ungreased baking sheet.
• Bake 12 to 15 minutes or until lightly browned.

*These little sandwiches can also be served for a heavy hors d'oeuvre. Use your imagination and make up interesting fillings.
Try sliced chicken with pineapple tidbits.
Turkey is good with Stilton or other blue cheese.*

## TURKEY AND CHEESE ROLLERS
### Yield: 2 sandwiches

2 rounds (10 inches each) soft flat bread or large,
    flour tortillas
4 tablespoons Dijon mustard or Horseradish Mayo
6 ounces smoked turkey, thinly sliced
1 cup Swiss or cheddar cheese, grated (about 4 ounces)
1 cup thinly shredded lettuce

• Place the flat bread on a cutting board and spread with
    2 tablespoons of mustard.
• Layer with half of the remaining ingredients.
• Starting at one end, roll up the sandwich as tightly as
    possible without tearing the bread.
• Slice in half, on the diagonal.
• Repeat with remaining flat bread and ingredients.

*Optional ingredients:*
    Ham and cheese
    Sliced olives or pickles
    Thinly sliced onions and bell peppers

HORSERADISH MAYO IS A GREAT SAUCE TO HAVE ON HAND FOR SANDWICHES.

STIR TOGETHER ½ CUP MAYONNAISE, ½ CUP SOUR CREAM, 1 TABLESPOON HORSERADISH, AND A DASH OF SALT. IT KEEPS 1 MONTH IN THE REFRIGERATOR.

MAKE UP YOUR OWN FILLINGS FOR THESE HANDY SANDWICHES. USE MONTEREY JACK CHEESE OR A COMBINATION OF CHEESES. ADD 2 TABLE-SPOONS GRATED BELL PEPPER, ¼ CUP CHOPPED HAM OR CHICKEN. FOR STUFFED TUNA AND CHEESE SANDWICHES, OMIT THE CHILIES AND OLIVES AND ADD 1 CAN (3 OUNCES) DRAINED TUNA.

# HOT STUFFED CHEESE ROLLS
## Yield: 12 sandwiches

2 cups grated cheddar cheese
2 tablespoons grated onion
1 can (3 ounces) chopped green chilies
1 can (3 ounces) sliced black olives
2 tablespoons minced cilantro, optional
2 tablespoons cider vinegar
2 tablespoons vegetable oil
2 drops Tabasco sauce
½ teaspoon Worcestershire sauce
1 package (12-count) small, prebaked sourdough rolls

• Preheat oven to 350°.
• Stir together all ingredients except the rolls.
• Use a serrated knife to cut ¼ inch off one short end of each roll. Use the knife to remove the inside bread from each roll, leaving a cavity for stuffing.
• Stuff each roll with cheese mixture. Reattach the end pieces, securing with toothpicks.
• Place on baking sheet and bake 20 minutes, or until hot and melted.

*These sandwiches are handy because they freeze well. Place in a freezer bag and then pull out the exact number you need. If time permits, allow to thaw at room temperature for 30 minutes before baking. If frozen, add 5 minutes to the baking time.*

*The two salads that follow are composed salads. Composed salads are arranged on a platter and then drizzled with dressing. Serve them with salad tongs so each person can make her own arrangement on her plate. The salads are hearty enough that crackers are all you need with them.*

## GREEK SALAD

Yield: 6 to 8 servings

*Greek salads are distinctive for containing olives, cucumbers, feta cheese, and lemon juice. You can add other family-favorite ingredients to the salad and make it very original.*

¾ pound fresh spinach, rinsed and sliced
1 small head red-tipped lettuce, sliced
4 Roma tomatoes, quartered
1 bell pepper, sliced
1 cucumber, peeled and thinly sliced
3 scallions, sliced
1 tablespoon dry oregano
¼ cup feta cheese crumbles
1 can artichoke hearts, drained
    and quartered
½ cup Greek or black pitted olives
¾ cup bottled Italian salad dressing
2 tablespoons lemon juice

• Place spinach and lettuce on a large platter.
• Arrange remaining salad ingredients on top.
• Whisk together the Italian dressing and lemon juice, and drizzle over salad.

## COBB SALAD
Yield: 4 servings

*If your family prefers, use cheddar cheese
in place of blue cheese in this recipe.*

¼ medium head iceberg lettuce, chopped, or 2 cups
1 medium head leafy green lettuce, torn into pieces
2 cups cooked chicken, diced
8 pieces bacon, cooked crisp and crumbled
8 ounces fresh mushrooms, washed and sliced
2 ripe tomatoes, diced
1 package (8 ounces) blue cheese crumbles,
or more, to taste
2 cups croutons
Oil and Vinegar Ranch Dressing

• Place lettuces on large platter.
• Arrange remaining salad ingredients on top.
• Drizzle with Oil and Vinegar Ranch Dressing.

## Tip

THIS SALAD
CAN BE MADE
WITH A VARIETY
OF COLD
SANDWICH
MEATS:
HAM, TURKEY,
BOLOGNA,
KIELBASA.
SERVE WITH
CRUSTY
SOURDOUGH
BREAD.

## MEAT AND CHEESE SALAD
Yield: 6 to 8 servings

⅓ pound salami, diced
⅓ pound spicy cooked sausage, diced
⅓ pound bierwurst, diced
1 medium red onion, sliced into thin rings
1 bunch green onions, sliced
1 red bell pepper, diced
½ pound mozzarella cheese, diced
1 bunch fresh basil, chopped
1 cup Parmesan cheese
3 cloves garlic, minced
2 cups olive oil
¾ cup balsamic vinegar

• Combine all ingredients except the garlic, olive oil,
and vinegar.
• In a small bowl, whisk together the garlic, olive oil,
and vinegar. Pour over the salad. Toss well.

## SMOKED TURKEY AND PEACH SALAD
### Yield: 4 to 6 servings
*Make this salad in the summer when peaches are plentiful.*

2 tablespoons white wine vinegar
1 tablespoon lemon juice
½ cup sour cream
2 tablespoons sugar
½ teaspoon salt
3 cups smoked turkey, thinly sliced
3 medium peaches or nectarines,
   peeled and sliced
1½ cups seedless green
   or red grapes, cut in half
4 ribs celery, thinly sliced
3 green onions, thinly sliced
½ cup peanuts

- Whisk together the vinegar,
  lemon juice, sour cream,
  sugar, and salt.
- Place remaining ingredients
  in a large bowl and drizzle with the dressing.
- Toss well.

## CORN AND BLACK BEAN SALAD
### Yield: 8 servings
*This is a beautiful salad and is great served with corn chips or corn bread.*

2 cans (15 ounces each) black beans, drained
2 cups frozen corn
4 green onions, sliced
1 medium red bell pepper, chopped
1 medium green bell pepper, chopped
1 bunch fresh cilantro, chopped
2 teaspoons minced garlic
$\frac{1}{4}$ cup lemon juice
2 tablespoons red wine vinegar
1 tablespoon chili powder
1 teaspoon salt
$\frac{1}{2}$ teaspoon pepper
$\frac{1}{2}$ cup vegetable oil

• In a large bowl, toss together the beans, corn, onions, peppers, cilantro, and garlic.
• Whisk together the lemon juice, vinegar, chili powder, salt, pepper, and oil.
• Pour dressing over salad and toss to coat well.

---

## CUCUMBER ONION SALAD
### Yield: 4 servings
*Use a carrot peeler to peel the cucumbers—quick and easy!*

1 large cucumber, peeled and thinly sliced
1 medium onion, peeled and thinly sliced
2 teaspoons salt
$\frac{1}{2}$ cup sour cream
1 tablespoon cider vinegar
2 drops Tabasco sauce
1 tablespoon dried dill
$\frac{1}{2}$ teaspoon pepper

• Place cucumber and onion slices in a large bowl and sprinkle with the salt.
• Allow to stand 30 minutes and then drain off the liquid.
• In a small bowl, combine remaining ingredients and fold into cucumbers and onions.
• Refrigerate at least 1 hour.

## HEARTY TUNA MACARONI SALAD
### Yield: 6 servings

6 ounces elbow or shell macaroni
1 can (12 ounces) tuna, drained
½ onion, grated or finely chopped
3 ribs celery, thinly sliced
¾ cup mayonnaise
Salt and pepper to taste

- Cook macaroni according to package directions; drain.
- Toss drained pasta with remaining ingredients until well mixed.
- Serve chilled or at room temperature.

*This salad was a Sunday tradition at my friend's when we were growing up. Her dad was a minister, and Sundays were workdays for their family. Her mom would make up this salad on Saturday, and it was even tastier from sitting overnight in the refrigerator! Make this when you have a big day and need to feed a lot of people.*

IF YOUR FAMILY BALKS AT MAYONNAISE, TRY STIRRING TOGETHER EQUAL PARTS MAYONNAISE AND SOUR CREAM, AND A TABLESPOON OF LEMON JUICE FOR A LIGHTER DRESSING.

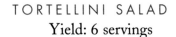

## TORTELLINI SALAD
### Yield: 6 servings

1½ pounds prepared tortellini
2 egg yolks
1 cup vegetable oil
¼ cup sour cream
3 tablespoons chopped fresh tarragon
1 tablespoon Dijon mustard
1 tablespoon tarragon or white wine vinegar

• Bring a large pot of salted water (1 tablespoon salt for 3 quarts of water) to a boil. When at a rolling boil, add the tortellini and cook until just tender (about 5 minutes).
• While the pasta is cooking, make the vinaigrette.
• Put the egg yolks in a mixing bowl and rapidly whisk the eggs while slowly dribbling in the oil.
• Whisk until thick and creamy.
• Stir in the remaining ingredients.
• Drain the pasta and immediately mix with vinaigrette.
• Serve warm, or cover and marinate in refrigerator for at least an hour.

## CHICKEN ALMOND SALAD
### Yield: 4 to 6 servings

4 cups cooked chicken, chopped
8 ribs celery, chopped
6 green onions, thinly sliced
¼ cup finely chopped onion
½ cup small pineapple chunks
1 cup slivered almonds
1 cup mayonnaise
½ teaspoon almond flavoring
1 teaspoon salt
½ teaspoon pepper

• Combine chicken, celery, onions, pineapple, and almonds.
• In a small bowl, combine mayonnaise, almond flavoring, salt, and pepper.
• Toss dressing gently with chicken mixture.

## CHINESE CHICKEN SALAD
### Yield: 6 servings

3 chicken breast halves, poached and shredded
1 head napa cabbage, shredded
2 cups honey-roasted peanuts or cashews
5 green onions, thinly sliced
1 cup crispy Chinese noodles

• Combine chicken, cabbage, peanuts, and green onions in a large bowl.
• In a jar with a tight-fitting lid, combine all dressing ingredients and shake well.
• Pour dressing over chicken salad mixture and toss well.
• Just before serving, sprinkle on crispy noodles and toss.

### *Dressing*
¼ cup vegetable oil, 1 tablespoon sesame oil
3 tablespoons rice vinegar, 2 tablespoons sugar
1 teaspoon soy sauce, 1½ teaspoons dry mustard
1 teaspoon grated fresh ginger

*Easy, Perfect Poached Chicken Breasts*

Place desired number of chicken breasts in a large saucepan or stockpot. Cover with enough water that chicken pieces have plenty of room and are not pressed together. (It is important that there is plenty of water.) Place over high heat and bring to a rolling boil. Remove from heat; cover, and allow to sit for 20 minutes. The chicken will be perfectly poached. This method works whether you have a small or large number of chicken breasts.

## CHICKEN APRICOT SALAD
### Yield: 6 to 8 servings

1 cup dried apricots, cut into 1/4-inch strips
1/2 cup apple or orange juice
3 pounds boneless chicken breasts, poached until tender, then sliced
1 cup sliced celery
4 or 5 green onions, sliced
3/4 cup slivered almonds, toasted
1/2 cup golden raisins
2 tablespoons minced fresh rosemary

• Place apricots and juice in a small saucepan and simmer gently for 2 minutes.
• In a large bowl, combine apricots and remaining salad ingredients.
• Pour on Honey Mustard Dressing and toss well.
• Serve chilled.

*This salad is a favorite at our cooking school. During the holidays, we add 1/2 cup dried cranberries in place of the raisins. Yellow raisins have enough sulfur added to the grapes in processing to keep them soft and light in color. They are more moist than dark raisins.*

## HONEY MUSTARD DRESSING
### Yield: 2 1/4 cups

1 egg or 1/4 cup egg substitute
2 tablespoons fresh lemon juice
2 tablespoons Dijon mustard
1 1/2 cups vegetable oil
1/4 cup honey mustard
Salt and pepper to taste

• Place the egg, lemon juice, and mustard in a food processor and process until smooth.
• With the machine running, drizzle in the oil very slowly to make a thick dressing.
• Stir in the honey mustard, salt, and pepper.

## CURRIED CHICKEN SALAD
### Yield 6 to 8 servings

¾ cup golden raisins
1 cup dry white wine or apple juice
1½ cups mayonnaise (fat-free is fine)
2 tablespoons lemon juice
1 tablespoon ground ginger
2 teaspoons curry powder
1 teaspoon salt
½ teaspoon pepper
6 chicken breast halves, poached and chopped
3 ribs celery, chopped
2 Granny Smith apples, chopped

- Place raisins and wine in a saucepan and simmer for 3 minutes.
- In a large bowl, whisk together the mayonnaise, lemon juice, ginger, curry powder, salt, and pepper.
- Add remaining ingredients, including raisins and liquid. Toss to coat well.

*Curried Chicken Salad would be delicious as a sandwich filling. For sandwiches, make sure all ingredients are chopped fine.*

NEW POTATOES
DON'T NEED
PEELING IF THE
SKINS ARE
TENDER AND
UNBLEMISHED.
IF YOU USE
RUSSET
POTATOES IN
THIS RECIPE,
PEEL THEM FIRST.

## FETA CHEESE POTATO SALAD
### Yield: 4 servings

2 pounds new potatoes
½ cup lemon juice (about 3 large lemons)
½ cup diced pimento
1 cup sliced black olives
1 bunch green onions, chopped
1 tablespoon dried oregano
½ cup olive oil
½ cup vegetable oil
Salt and pepper to taste
4 ounces feta cheese

- Wash the potatoes but do not peel them. Cut away any bad places and cut them into halves.
- Place in a large saucepan. Cover with water and simmer gently until just tender, about 20 minutes.
- When just cool enough to handle, cut potatoes into bite-sized chunks and place in a large bowl.
- Sprinkle warm potatoes with ¼ cup lemon juice and stir in pimentos, olives, onions, and oregano.
- In a small bowl, combine remaining lemon juice, olive oil, and vegetable oil. Whisk to combine. Add to potatoes. Stir in salt and pepper.
- Fold in cheese. Refrigerate until ready to serve.

*Feta cheese is traditionally made from ewe's milk, but American feta cheese is made from cow's milk. A soft, crumbly cheese with a tangy flavor, it is often sold in crumbles or in a square packed in brine.*

## POTATO AND SUGAR SNAP PEA SALAD
### Yield: 6 to 8 servings
*Oriental snow peas can be used in place of sugar snap.*

2 pounds new potatoes, washed
　and cut into bite-sized pieces
2 tablespoons balsamic vinegar
　or red wine vinegar
Juice and zest of 1 large lemon
　(3 tablespoons juice)
1/3 cup vegetable oil
1/2 teaspoon sugar
Salt and pepper to taste
1 small red onion, cut into thin rings
1 pound sugar snap peas, ends trimmed

- Boil potatoes in salted water until just tender,
　about 7 minutes.
- Drain potatoes and place in a large bowl.
- Meanwhile, whisk together the vinegar, lemon juice,
　zest, oil, sugar, salt, and pepper.
- Add to the potatoes, along with the onions and sugar snap peas.

*This is one of my son's favorite salads.*
*It was always nice to have a big bowl made up*
*in the refrigerator for him to dig into when he needed a snack.*

## MOM'S POTATO SALAD
### Yield: 10 to 12 servings

*This is a great, basic potato salad recipe. To make it your own special mixture, add what you especially like in potato salads, like chopped hard-cooked eggs, pickle relish, chopped bell peppers, or pimentos.*

8 new potatoes, washed but not peeled
1½ cups mayonnaise
1 cup sour cream
1½ teaspoons prepared horseradish
1 teaspoon celery seed
1 teaspoon salt
¼ teaspoon pepper
½ cup fresh, chopped parsley
1 cup finely chopped onion

- Cut potatoes in half. Place in a large saucepan and cover with water. Add salt. Cover and boil until just tender, about 15 minutes. Drain.
- When potatoes are just cool enough to handle, cut them into bite-sized pieces and combine with remaining ingredients in a large bowl. Refrigerate for several hours.

*Horseradish is a root vegetable and has a very spicy flavor. It is often served as a condiment with meat, such as prime rib. Prepared horseradish is finely grated and is available in a jar. Adding a little to potato salad makes subtle yet delicious "extra" flavor.*

## SWEET MARINATED SLAW
### Yield: 12 servings

1 head (3 pounds) green cabbage, thinly shredded
1 bell pepper, shredded
1½ cups shredded onion
2 cups sugar
1 cup vegetable oil
2 tablespoons celery seed
2 tablespoons salt

• Combine cabbage, bell pepper, and onion in a large
salad bowl. Set aside.
• In a saucepan, combine remaining ingredients. Cook and
stir until the sugar is dissolved and the mixture is hot.
• Pour over cabbage mixture and stir well. Cool slaw;
cover and refrigerate at least 4 hours.

## SAUERKRAUT SALAD
### Yield: 8 servings
*I loved this specialty of my grandmother's as I was growing up.
Use it as a side dish for any meal, and create memories.*

¼ cup cider vinegar
¼ cup water
1 cup sugar
1 can (16 ounces) sauerkraut, well drained
1 onion, finely chopped
2 stalks celery, finely chopped
1 bell pepper, finely chopped
2 tablespoons chopped pimento

• In a saucepan, combine the vinegar, water, and sugar.
Bring to a simmer.
• Cook and stir until sugar is dissolved, about 2 minutes.
• Combine remaining ingredients in a large bowl.
• Pour hot dressing over and stir well.
• Cover and chill at least 4 hours.
• Store in the refrigerator up to 2 weeks.

THINLY SHREDDED CABBAGE IS ONE SECRET TO MAKING REALLY GREAT SLAW. SHREDDING CABBAGE IS A SNAP IF YOU HAVE A FOOD PROCESSOR. BUT IF NOT, DON'T WORRY! IT IS A FUN AND REALLY EASY JOB. FIRST, CUT THE ENTIRE HEAD IN HALF AND PLACE ONE HALF, FLAT SIDE DOWN, ON A CUTTING BOARD. USE A LARGE FRENCH KNIFE TO MAKE THIN SLICES. KEEP TURNING THE CABBAGE SO THE KNIFE EASILY SLICES. THE SLICES DON'T HAVE TO BE LONG PIECES; THEY CAN BE SHORT SHREDS. THE IDEA IS THAT THE CABBAGE IS PAPER-THIN—IT'S MORE FUN TO EAT THAT WAY!

## Fun Salad

*This is one of those "throw-together" lifesavers I have used many times. The secret to making it fun to eat is slivering the iceberg lettuce. All ingredients are chopped small, and it can be piled on saltine crackers as you eat it. With the tuna and vegetables, it is a perfect "one-dish" spring or summer meal!*

### SLIVERED ICEBERG AND TUNA SALAD
Yield: 4 to 6 servings

½ head iceberg lettuce
3 green onions, chopped or sliced
½ bell pepper, chopped
1 can (4 ounces) sliced black olives
1 jar (2 ounces) chopped pimentos
1 cup frozen peas, thawed (They will thaw while you make the salad.)
1 can (6 ounces) tuna, drained
1 recipe Lemon Ranch Dressing

• To sliver the lettuce, lay it flat side down on a cutting board and use a large French knife to make small slices, turning the lettuce as you slice.
• In a large bowl, toss together all salad ingredients. Drizzle on dressing to taste.
• Serve with saltine crackers.

---

### JULIE'S FAVORITE GREEN SALAD
Yield: 8 servings
*My niece Julie is asked to bring this salad to all family gatherings. We are all hooked on it!*

1 head romaine or leafy green lettuce
8 ounces Swiss cheese, grated
1 pound fresh mushrooms, sliced
8 ounces sliced almonds, toasted

Combine all salad ingredients and toss with dressing.

*Dressing:*
1 package dry Good Seasons Italian Salad Dressing mix
3 tablespoons balsamic vinegar
½ cup vegetable oil
Juice of one large lemon (about 3 tablespoons)

• Place all ingredients in a jar and shake well.

## ORIENTAL PEA SALAD
### Yield: 8 servings

4 cups fresh or frozen green peas
6 scallions, finely chopped
1 can (8 ounces) sliced water chestnuts, drained
1¼ cups honey-roasted cashews
1 cup sour cream
1 tablespoon minced fresh ginger
2 tablespoons soy sauce
2 teaspoons sesame oil
2 teaspoons light brown sugar
2 tablespoons chopped cilantro

- If using fresh peas, blanch or steam until crisp-tender, 3 to 4 minutes.
  Drain and cool under cold running water.
- In a large mixing bowl, combine peas, scallions, water chestnuts, and cashews.
- In a small bowl, whisk together the sour cream, ginger, soy sauce, sesame oil,
  brown sugar, and cilantro.
- Pour dressing over the pea salad and stir well.
- Cover and refrigerate until time to serve.

## CHICKEN AND ARTICHOKE RICE SALAD
### Yield: 8 servings

1 package (6 ounces) wild rice mix
¼ cup sliced green, stuffed olives
2 chicken breast halves, cooked and sliced into ½-inch pieces
¼ teaspoon curry powder
½ cup mayonnaise
½ green pepper, chopped
Salt and pepper to taste
2 jars (6 ounces each) marinated artichoke hearts,
   coarsely chopped, with marinade
2 scallions, chopped

- Cook the rice according to package directions and allow to cool.
- In a large bowl, combine all ingredients and stir well.
- Serve very cold.

*Once, when a friend went unexpectedly to the hospital, my daughter and I dashed into the grocery store and ran in two directions to grab ingredients for the Five-Cup Fruit Salad. We met at the checkout in less than 5 minutes! We took this salad to our friend's family that night, along with a roasted chicken.*

## FIVE-CUP FRUIT SALAD
### Yield: 4 servings
*Five-Cup Fruit Salad is easy to remember.
Just grab these five ingredients!*

1 cup pineapple chunks, drained
1 cup mandarin oranges, drained
1 cup coconut
1 cup miniature marshmallows
1 cup sour cream

• Stir together all ingredients.
• Refrigerate at least 2 hours or until chilled.

## HEAVENLY FRUIT AND RICE SALAD
### Yield: 4 to 6 servings
*This rice salad works well with leftover rice,
so the next time you are cooking rice,
fix extra to have on hand.*

1 cup pineapple chunks, drained
$\frac{1}{4}$ cup maraschino cherries, chopped
1 cup mandarin oranges, drained
1 cup cooked, cooled rice
$\frac{1}{4}$ teaspoon almond flavoring
2 cups whipped cream or whipped topping

• Stir together all ingredients.
• Refrigerate at least 2 hours or until chilled.

## MIXED FRUIT BOWL
### Yield: 8 servings

1 can (7 ounces) sliced peaches with juice
1 can (7 ounces) apricot halves with juice
1 can (7 ounces) pineapple chunks
$\frac{1}{4}$ cup maraschino cherries
1 banana, sliced
$\frac{1}{4}$ teaspoon almond flavoring

• Mix together and chill.

*Unexpected lunch guests? No problem! Throw this salad together, and put it in the freezer to chill while you fix a few quick sandwiches. Better yet—keep cans of fruit in the refrigerator for emergencies like this!*

## FROZEN FRUIT CUPS
### Yield: 18 fruit cups

3 bananas, mashed with a fork
1 can (15 ounces) apricots
1 can (15 ounces) sliced peaches
1 box (10 ounces) frozen strawberries
1 cup sugar
$\frac{1}{2}$ cup water
3 drops red food coloring

• Line 18 muffin tins with paper cupcake liners.
• Combine mashed bananas and undrained fruit in a large bowl.
• In a saucepan, combine sugar and water. Cook, stirring to dissolve sugar, about 2 minutes. Pour over fruit. Stir in red food coloring.
• Fill each cupcake liner with mixture. Freeze.
• To serve, remove from freezer and peel off paper.
Place frozen fruit cup on a lettuce leaf.

*You may want to use other canned fruits, such as fruit cocktail, in this recipe. Add one-fourth cup chopped maraschino cherries for more color, if desired.*

*Take the time to make this salad, and you will have a special treat for several meals. It keeps 3 to 4 days in the refrigerator.*

## LAYERED STRAWBERRY CREAM GELATIN SALAD
### Yield: 10 to 12 servings

1 package (6 ounces) strawberry gelatin
1 cup boiling water
1 package (10 ounces) frozen strawberries, thawed
1 can (28 ounces) crushed pineapple
3 bananas, mashed with a fork
1 cup chopped pecans, optional
2 cups sour cream (fat-free is fine)

- Dissolve gelatin in boiling water.
- Stir in berries, pineapple (with juice), bananas, and pecans.
- Pour half of this mixture into 9 x 13-inch baking dish.
- Refrigerate until firm, about 3 hours.
- When firm, spread evenly with sour cream, and then gently spoon remaining gelatin mixture over all.
- Refrigerate until well set, about 3 hours.

## APRICOT FLUFF
### Yield: 8 servings

1 container (16 ounces) frozen whipped topping, thawed
1 can sweetened condensed milk (fat-free is fine)
1 can (20 ounces) crushed pineapple, drained
1 can apricot pie filling
1 cup small marshmallows
1 cup chopped pecans

- Stir together all ingredients and pile into your favorite serving bowl.
- Refrigerate until ready to serve.

## BING CHERRY SALAD
### Yield: 6 to 8 servings

2 eggs, beaten
2 tablespoons sugar
⅓ cup lemon juice
2 tablespoons butter
2 cups miniature marshmallows
1 can (17 ounces) pineapple chunks, drained
1 can (17 ounces) Bing cherries, drained
1 cup chopped pecans, optional
2 cups whipped cream or whipped topping

• Place eggs, sugar, and lemon juice in a saucepan.
  Stir to combine.
• Place over low heat and cook, stirring constantly until
  mixture thickens.
• Remove from heat and stir in butter and marshmallows.
• Cool mixture.
• Fold in drained pineapple, cherries, and pecans. Fold in
  whipped cream.
• Pile into two-quart bowl and refrigerate 4 hours or
  overnight.

*Let your children help you make this salad, and take it to a family who needs a dinner. It not only tastes good, but with all the special ingredients, it is a cheerful salad!*

## POPPY SEED DRESSING
### Yield: 3 cups
*Great on any salad, especially Field Greens with Bacon and Sugared Pecans.*

1½ cups sugar
2 teaspoons dry mustard
2 teaspoons salt
⅔ cup white vinegar
1 tablespoon grated onion
2 cups vegetable oil
2 tablespoons poppy seeds

• Place sugar, mustard, salt, vinegar, and grated onion in a blender.
• Blend until smooth.
• With blender running, slowly dribble in the vegetable oil.
• Stir in poppy seeds.

---

### DOUBLE BOILERS

*If you don't have a double boiler, place a small saucepan inside a larger one and fill the bottom pan with one inch of water. Cooking in a double boiler gives a gentle heat for foods that are easily overcooked. In this recipe the eggs would scramble if cooked too hot.*

## COOKED ORANGE SALAD DRESSING
### Yield: 1½ cups
*This dressing is fabulous on fresh fruit of any kind and makes a mixed fruit salad extraspecial.*

1 cup sugar
1 egg
Zest and juice of one large orange
Zest and juice of one large lemon

• Place all ingredients in the top of a double boiler and cook and stir until thick, about 5 minutes.
• Refrigerate until cold.

## BALSAMIC MAPLE VINAIGRETTE
Yield: about 2¼ cups

½ cup balsamic vinegar
¼ cup pure maple syrup
1 large shallot, minced
1 cup vegetable oil
½ cup olive oil
½ teaspoon salt
¼ teaspoon pepper

• Place all ingredients in a large jar with a tight-fitting lid.
• Shake to mix well.
• Refrigerate until needed; shake before using.

IT'S SO EASY TO PREPARE SALAD DRESSING IN A QUART JAR. YOU CAN PUT IT DIRECTLY INTO THE REFRIGERATOR. TO USE, SIMPLY SHAKE WELL AND POUR.

## CELERY SEED DRESSING
Yield: 2¼ cups

1 tablespoon minced onion
1 teaspoon salt
1 teaspoon celery seed
2 teaspoons paprika
1 cup sugar
½ cup cider vinegar
1 cup vegetable oil

• Place all ingredients in a quart jar and shake.
Or place in a bowl and whisk until smooth.
• Store in the refrigerator up to 1 month.

## SWEET BASIL VINAIGRETTE
Yield: about 3 cups

2 cups vegetable oil
1 cup red wine vinegar
¼ cup Worcestershire sauce
1 tablespoon dried parsley
1 tablespoon dried, crushed basil
3 teaspoons salt
1 teaspoon pepper

• Place all ingredients in 1-quart canning jar and shake well.
• Store in the refrigerator up to 1 month.
• Shake just before using.

## MEXICAN RANCH DRESSING
Yield: 2 cups

1½ cups prepared ranch dressing
½ cup salsa

• Stir ingredients together until well mixed.

## BLUE CHEESE RANCH DRESSING
Yield: 1 cup

Prepare Oil and Vinegar Ranch Dressing, adding 2 ounces (¼ cup)
blue cheese crumbles and 1 teaspoon minced garlic.

## SWEET AND SOUR DRESSING
Yield: about 2 cups

¼ cup cider vinegar
⅓ cup ketchup
2 tablespoons Worcestershire sauce
½ cup sugar
2 tablespoons grated onion
1 teaspoon minced garlic
1 cup vegetable oil

• Place all ingredients in a jar and shake well.

## THOUSAND ISLAND DRESSING
Yield: about 2 cups

1½ cups mayonnaise
½ cup ketchup
¼ cup sweet pickle relish
¼ cup grated onion
Juice of one lemon (2 tablespoons)
Salt and pepper to taste

• Stir together all ingredients.

## OIL AND VINEGAR RANCH DRESSING
Yield: about 1 cup

1 package (1 ounce) dry ranch dressing mix
¼ cup vinegar
3 tablespoons water
½ cup vegetable oil

• Place all ingredients in a jar and shake well.

## CREAMY BLUE CHEESE DRESSING
### Yield: 1 quart

2 cups mayonnaise
1 cup sour cream
2 tablespoons lemon juice
1 tablespoon Worcestershire sauce
1 teaspoon minced garlic or to taste
$\frac{1}{4}$ cup grated onion, optional
12 ounces blue cheese
Salt and pepper to taste

• Combine all ingredients and stir until creamy. Dressing will be lumpy with cheese.
• Store in the refrigerator up to 1 week.

## FRENCH DRESSING
### Yield: about 3½ cups

2 cups vegetable oil
1 cup white wine vinegar
$\frac{1}{4}$ cup Worcestershire sauce
1 tablespoon dried parsley
1 tablespoon dried basil
3 teaspoons salt
1 teaspoon pepper

• Place all ingredients in 1-quart jar and shake well.

## LEMON RANCH DRESSING
### Yield: about 1 cup

Prepare Oil and Vinegar Ranch Dressing,
using $\frac{1}{4}$ cup lemon juice in place of vinegar.

## HOMEMADE CARIBBEAN SALAD DRESSING
Yield: 1½ cups

¼ cup cider vinegar
⅓ cup ketchup
½ cup sugar
2 tablespoons Worcestershire sauce
1 tablespoon grated onion
1 teaspoon minced garlic
1 cup vegetable oil

• Combine all ingredients in a quart jar and shake.
• Store in the refrigerator up to 2 months. Shake each time just before serving.

---

## MAYONNAISE
Yield: about 1½ cups mayonnaise
*Homemade mayonnaise will keep 5 to 6 days, tightly covered,
in the refrigerator.*

1 egg
1 tablespoon lemon juice
1 tablespoon brown mustard
¼ teaspoon salt
1¼ cups vegetable oil

*For a quick seafood
sauce, add
2 tablespoons
pickle relish,
1 tablespoon catsup,
and salt and pepper
to taste.*

• In the bowl of a food processor, whip the egg, lemon juice, mustard, and salt.
• With processor running, slowly dribble in the oil.
• As the mixture emulsifies, it will become thick and smooth.

*Knowing how to throw together mayonnaise will help
make many dishes extra special for your family.
It is delicious on top of hot green beans.
It makes sandwiches really tasty. Stir in capers, chopped scallions,
pickle relish, or horseradish to make an unusual condiment for meats,
freshly steamed vegetables, or as a topping for baked potatoes.*

## QUICK
### BREAD AND BUTTER PICKLES
### Yield: 4 quarts

*These pickles are fun to make, and everyone loves them.*

2 cups white vinegar
$6\frac{1}{2}$ cups sugar
1 gallon jar of whole dill or sour pickles

• Combine vinegar and sugar in a nonmetallic bowl.
Stir to dissolve.
• Drain pickles and discard liquid.
• Slice pickles into desired thickness and place back
in empty gallon jar.
• Pour vinegar mixture over pickles.
This mixture will be very thick, and the sugar
won't be completely dissolved. This is okay.
• Place the lid securely on the gallon jar
and place the pickles in the refrigerator for 5 days.
• Each day, turn the jar upside down a few times
until the sugar is completely dissolved.
• Pack into smaller jars, if desired, for gift giving.

# CHAPTER THREE
## Dinner

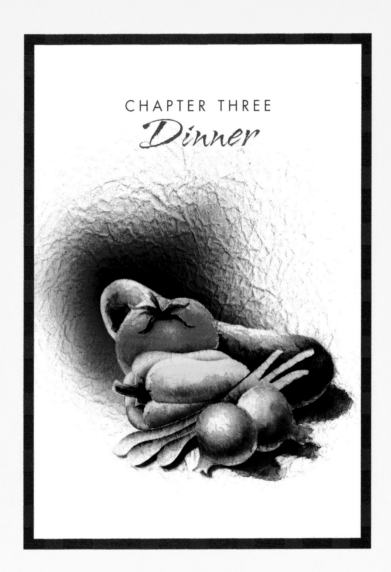

# "What's for dinner, Mom?"

*How many* times do you hear this each week? And for the first time all day, there is a hush among the troops as everyone waits for your big announcement. But, hey, didn't you just fill them up last night? They're hungry again? Story of your life!

It can be frustrating trying to keep up with all these meals. You need ideas! And you need a game plan that makes a week of suppers a somewhat organized series of events. Why not use this book to cut down on that last-minute frantic feeling that makes you crave antacids?

With a few tricks up your sleeve, you can create a list of weekly evening menus that will help take some of the stress out of dinnertime. Follow these meal-planning tips:

1. Designate a day each week when you sit down with paper and pencil and spend time organizing a week's worth of menus. A good day might be the one when your newspaper runs grocery ads and specials. Keep your menu handy for the week.

2. Give each weekday a "food identity" and name that food for that day. Here is an example: Monday, Mexican or Oriental food; Tuesday, pasta; Wednesday, chicken or pork dish; Thursday, quiche or beef dish; Friday, fish or grilled meat; Saturday, soup or stew; Sunday, roasted chicken. Go through your recipes and choose one for each day to match that day's "food identity." This simplifies the choices.

3. Make a habit of organizing the ingredients for dinner before you start your day. Take meat out of the freezer, set out canned goods, or chop a salad (cover and refrigerate). This takes away that five o'clock feeling of despair when you realize that evening's chicken is a frozen brick.

4. Be flexible! If your son's big ball game ends up falling at four o'clock on Tamale Pie Monday, this might be the time to grab fast-food tacos and keep the pie for another day. Remember now that your children's dinner-time memories will last a lifetime. It's more important to laugh together than have a perfect meal.

# Survival Pantry

### REFRIGERATOR:

Butter
Mayonnaise
Ketchup
Dijon mustard
Yeast
Minced garlic
Jalapenos
Prepared piecrusts
Lettuce
Broccoli
Lemons
Bell peppers

### FROZEN PANTRY:

Ground beef
Chicken pieces
Fish fillets
Beef ribs
Crabmeat
Grated cheddar cheese
Frozen vegetables: green peas,
    new potatoes, snow peas, corn,
    okra
Raspberries
Bread

### FRESH VEGETABLES
### AND FRUIT:

Potatoes
Onions
Tomatoes
Bananas
Apples

### DRY PANTRY:

Flour
Cornmeal
Corn bread mix
Pasta, noodles, rice, dried barley
Instant oatmeal
Raisin bran cereal
Gelatin—orange and raspberry
Sugar, brown and white
Vegetable oil, olive oil
Vinegar cider, red wine
Ranch dressing mix
Bottled Caesar dressing
Salsa
Condiments: pickles, relish, olives,
    pimentos

### CANNED ITEMS:

Diced tomatoes
Green beans, artichoke hearts
Chopped green chilies
Bing cherries

### HERBS AND SPICES:

Parsley
Sage
Rosemary
Thyme
Basil
Cinnamon
Sugar

# A Month of Dinner Menus

## WEEK #1

Monday: Aunt Jan's Tamale Pie, shredded lettuce with
  Mexican Ranch Dressing

Tuesday: Chicken and Dumplings, Bing Cherry Salad,
  Cheese Toast

Wednesday: Stuffed Pork Tenderloin, green beans,
  sourdough bread slices

Thursday: Mom's Shortcut Meat Loaf, baked potatoes
  (bake extra for Saturday), tossed salad

Friday: Crab and Artichoke Casserole, buttered green peas,
  sliced tomatoes

Saturday: Baked Potato Soup, Green Chile and Cheese Corn Bread

Sunday: Chicken in a Bag, steamed broccoli with lemon,
  Angel Biscuits

## WEEK #2

Monday: Chicken Oriental, frozen snow peas with lemon butter

Tuesday: Chicken Spaghetti Casserole

Wednesday: Juicy ribs, Mom's Potato Salad,
  bread with butter

Thursday: Judie's Easy Cheesy Quiche, fresh fruit salad with
  Poppy Seed Dressing

Friday: Hamburgers on the grill

Saturday: Tomato Basil Pie, Caesar Salad

Sunday: Parsley, Sage, Rosemary, and Thyme Roasted Chicken,
  buttered new potatoes (use frozen ones), Slow-Cooked Fresh Green Beans
  (cook on Saturday and reheat)

## WEEK #3

Monday: Hearty and Wonderful Chicken and Rice, tossed salad
Tuesday: Italian Chicken and Pasta, steamed yellow squash
  or buttered peas
Wednesday: Quick Chicken Cacciatore, buttered noodles,
  green salad
Thursday: Beef and Noodle Casserole, Shelly Beans,
  Oatmeal Muffins
Friday: Crispy Fish Nuggets, Cheesy Baked Asparagus,
  Frozen Fruit Cups
Saturday: Mom's World Famous Vegetable Soup,
  Cheese Toast
Sunday: Roasted Rosemary Chicken, Colorful Corn
  and Okra

## WEEK #4

Monday: Fire Station Jalapeno Chicken, buttered rice
Tuesday: Baked Pasta with Spinach, Cheese, and Tomatoes,
  tossed green salad, and Garlicky Toast
Wednesday: Cobb Salad, Raisin Bran Muffins
Thursday: Beef Stroganoff, buttered noodles, fresh fruit salad
Friday: Grilled chicken, Julie's Favorite Green Salad
Saturday: Vegetable Beef and Barley Soup,
  Orange Corn Muffins
Sunday: Very Easy Baked Game Hens,
  Broccoli and Cheese Casserole

*This delicious version of corn bread is very moist and is usually spooned from its baking dish. I'll bet it becomes a favorite with your family!*

## MEXICAN SPOON BREAD
### Yield: 8 servings

3 eggs
1 cup buttermilk
½ cup butter, melted
1 cup frozen corn
1 can (2 ounces) chopped green chilies
1 cup cornmeal
3 teaspoons baking powder
½ teaspoon salt
1½ cups grated Monterey Jack cheese

- Preheat oven to 350°. Spray an 8-inch baking dish with vegetable oil.
- In a mixing bowl, beat together the eggs and buttermilk.
- Stir in the corn and green chilies.
- Combine cornmeal, baking powder, and salt in a large bowl.
- Add to the liquid mixture, mixing just until dry ingredients are moistened; do not overmix.
- Pour mixture into prepared baking dish.
- Sprinkle the cheese over the top.
- Bake 45 minutes or until top is golden brown.

## MOM'S CORN BREAD
### Yield: 6 to 8 servings

1 cup cornmeal
1 cup flour
¼ cup sugar
4 teaspoons baking powder
1 teaspoon salt
1 egg
1 cup milk
¼ cup vegetable oil

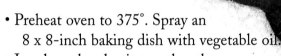

- Preheat oven to 375°. Spray an
  8 x 8-inch baking dish with vegetable oil.
- In a large bowl, stir together the
  dry ingredients.
- Add remaining ingredients and stir
  until well mixed.
- Pour into prepared pan.
- Bake 25 minutes or until golden brown.

## VINTAGE PAN

If you can find a vintage aluminum omelette pan, also called a camp pan, you will enjoy making corn bread on top of the stove—especially in the hot months when you don't want to heat the oven.

Spray the omelette pan with vegetable oil, and place it on the stove over medium heat. When hot, fill ⅔ full with batter. Reduce heat to low. Close pan and cook 12 to 15 minutes on first side. Then flip the pan over and cook 10 to 12 minutes on second side, or until bread is done.

## GREEN CHILE AND CHEESE CORN BREAD
Yield: 6 to 8 servings

1 cup cornmeal
1 teaspoon salt
½ teaspoon baking soda
1 can (17 ounces) creamed corn
½ cup minced onion
¼ cup salad oil
2 eggs
1½ cups grated cheddar cheese
1 can (4 ounces) diced green chilies

• Preheat oven to 375°. Spray an 8 x 8-inch baking dish with vegetable oil.
• In a large bowl, stir together the cornmeal, salt, and baking soda.
• Stir in remaining ingredients.
• Pour batter into prepared baking dish.
• Bake 45 minutes.

## ORANGE CORN MUFFINS
Yield: 6 muffins

1 package (6 ounces) corn bread mix
1 tablespoon orange zest
¼ cup chopped pecans

• Prepare corn bread mix according to package directions.
• Lightly stir in orange zest and pecans.
• Bake according to package directions.

## QUICK MUFFINS
Yield: 12 muffins

2 cups self-rising flour
1 cup sour cream
½ cup butter or margarine, melted
½ cup milk

• Preheat oven to 375°.
• Line 12 muffin cups with muffin papers or spray with vegetable oil.
• Mix all ingredients together until a smooth batter is formed.
• Fill muffin cups.
• Bake 15 minutes or until golden brown.

# ANGEL BISCUITS
## Yield: 16 rolls
*These rolls don't have to rise before baking,
but it won't hurt if they do rise a little.*

5 cups flour
3 teaspoons baking powder
¼ cup sugar
1 teaspoon baking soda
1 teaspoon salt
¾ cup vegetable shortening
1 package yeast
¼ cup warm water
2 cups buttermilk
½ cup butter, melted and cooled

- Preheat oven to 375°.
- Stir together all dry ingredients.
- Use a pastry cutter or two forks to cut in shortening until evenly distributed and crumbly.
- Dissolve yeast in warm water and then add to buttermilk.
- Add buttermilk mixture to dry ingredients and mix well. (At this point the dough can be covered and refrigerated until needed, up to 3 weeks.)
- Roll dough ½-inch thick and cut out biscuits with a biscuit cutter or knife.
- Roll each biscuit in melted butter and place in baking dish.
- Bake 12 to 15 minutes or until golden brown.

*The Angel Biscuit recipe is fabulous
as dinner rolls, as cinnamon rolls,
or stuffed with ham on a buffet table.*

THIS DOUGH IS GREAT FOR BUSY COOKS BECAUSE IT CAN BE STORED UP TO 3 WEEKS IN THE REFRIGERATOR. SIMPLY CUT OFF THE AMOUNT YOU NEED FOR DINNER. THE RESULT? FRESHLY BAKED BREAD WITHOUT MIXING DOUGH!

# Eat Your Vegetables!

*Why is* it kids don't crave vegetables? Why couldn't they turn up their noses at candy instead? Unfortunately, that will never happen. You will have an easier time convincing your kids to eat vegetables if they are prepared in a fun way. Here are some tips on cooking vegetables:

*Frozen:* Except for green beans, most vegetables taste great when you buy them frozen and follow package directions. Green beans seem to be tough and have a strange taste when frozen; they are better from the can.

*Canned:* Spinach and peas aren't the best when canned. They are better frozen. Canned asparagus is best if served very cold as a salad, with lemon juice. Everything else is okay canned; just don't heat too long, or the vegetables will get mushy and lose their color.

*Cooking fresh vegetables:* Green vegetables will keep their green color if they are cooked less than 7 to 9 minutes.

Steaming is usually best. Use the common metal basket of overlapping metal leaves that converts saucepans into steamers.

Boiling is fine too, but vegetables get waterlogged if boiled too long.

Sautéing is great. Cut large vegetables into bite-sized pieces and toss in a little oil over high heat.

Dry baking works for potatoes, but most vegetables don't have enough moisture and need to be drizzled with oil first.

Grilling seems to make vegetables more appealing to children since they like to see tasty favorites such as hot dogs and hamburgers come off the grill. Most vegetables are best when drizzled with oil and wrapped in foil.

*Quick toppings for vegetables:* Lemon juice is tasty on all vegetables. Serve lemon quarters and let your kids squeeze on their own juice. Horseradish sauce makes broccoli or green beans more interesting. Dill Dip is a favorite for dipping raw vegetables such as carrots, celery, zucchini, and cucumber slices. It is also delicious on cooked vegetables. Serve it in a bowl next to a platter of assorted steamed veggies.

I hope these vegetable recipes help you add interest and fun to your dinners!

## ARTICHOKES

Pull off the rough outer leaves and slice off the stem at the base. Use a serrated knife to slice off the top ½ inch, removing the useless thorny top. Use kitchen scissors to trim the tops off each of the outer leaves. If desired, rub all cut surfaces with lemon juice to prevent browning.

To cook, place artichokes upside down in a large pot and cover halfway with water. Sprinkle on 1 teaspoon salt for each artichoke in the pot. Cover and simmer 20 minutes or until the stem end is tender and the outer leaves are loose.

Use tongs to remove artichokes from the water and let them drain a few minutes before placing on serving plates. Serve with Lemon Butter.

## LEMON BUTTER

For each serving, melt ¼ cup butter and stir in 2 tablespoons lemon juice. To eat, pull off leaves, dip in butter and scrape off the soft inner meat with your teeth. Place eaten leaves, scraped-side down, on your plate.

When you get to the bristly choke, use a paring knife to cut a cone-shaped wedge, removing the choke. What's left underneath is the artichoke's heart—the best part! Cut up and dip in the Lemon Butter!

*Eating artichokes with Lemon Butter for dipping was always a treat when we were raising our kids. Teach your children how to cut out the choke and get to the grand prize—the heart!*

*Artichokes are the blossoms of a large thistle plant grown mainly in California. Fields of these gray-green plants stretch to the horizon in every direction. They are harvested mainly in the springtime and are available year-round. They contain about 44 calories each. (It's the butter that gets you!)*

*Choose artichokes with firm, solid heads and compact leaves. If the leaves are brown, the artichokes have been in storage too long.*

TO TRIM
ASPARAGUS,
TAKE ONE OF THE
THICKEST STEMS
AND HOLD IT
BETWEEN THE
FINGERS OF BOTH
HANDS AND BEND
IT UNTIL IT
SNAPS. THIS WILL
TELL YOU WHERE
THE STEMS BEGIN
TO GET TOUGH.
THEN ON A
CUTTING BOARD,
LAY THE OTHER
STEMS NEXT TO
THE SNAPPED ONE
AND USE A LARGE
KNIFE TO SLICE
THEM SO THEY
ARE THE SAME
LENGTH AS THE
SNAPPED ONE.
QUICK AND
EASY—READY
TO COOK!

## CHEESY BAKED ASPARAGUS
### Yield: 4 servings

2 pounds fresh asparagus, washed and trimmed
½ cup melted butter
1 envelope dry onion soup mix
1 cup grated mozzarella or cheddar cheese

- Preheat oven to 450°.
- Lay the asparagus in a baking dish.
- Stir together the melted butter and soup mix. Pour over the asparagus. Top with cheese.
- Bake 10 minutes or until cheese is melted.

*Asparagus is a sure sign of spring, since this is when it pops up out of the ground and is ready to pick from the garden. The best way to wash it is to fill the sink with water and swish asparagus carefully for a few seconds. Empty the sink. If there is any sand on the bottom, repeat the process.*

## GRILLED ASPARAGUS
### Yield: 4 servings

1½ to 2 pounds fresh asparagus, washed and trimmed
2 tablespoons vegetable or olive oil
Salt and pepper to taste
Lemon wedges

- Preheat gas grill or prepare a charcoal fire.
- Place asparagus on a platter and drizzle with oil. Sprinkle with salt and pepper.
- When fire is hot, place asparagus spears directly on heated grill and cook, turning the spears midway, about 10 minutes or until heated through and tender.
- Serve with lemon wedges.

## BUTTERY GREEN PEAS
## AND PEARL ONIONS
Yield: 4 servings

3 cups frozen peas
2 cups frozen pearl onions
1 teaspoon salt, or to taste
½ teaspoon pepper
1 tablespoon butter, or to taste

• Place peas, onions, and salt in a saucepan and add about 1 inch of water.
• Cover and simmer 3 to 4 minutes.
• Drain water, add pepper and butter, and toss to coat well.

## BARBECUE BAKED BEANS
Yield: 10 to 12 servings

8 pieces bacon, cut into slivers
1½ cups chopped onion
1 cup chopped green bell pepper
2 cans (28 ounces) baked beans
1 cup brown sugar
1 cup ketchup
¼ cup Worcestershire sauce

• Preheat oven to 350°.
• In a large skillet, cook the bacon until it is transparent.
• Add the chopped onion and bell pepper.
Cook, stirring for 5 minutes until onion is soft.
• Place beans in a 3-quart baking dish.
Stir in cooked bacon mixture and all remaining ingredients.
• Cover and bake 2 hours.
• Uncover and bake another ½ hour.

*Beans might be somewhat soupy when done
but will thicken up after you take them out of the oven.*

## Ham Hocks

*Ham hocks are found in the meat department at your grocery store.*
*I usually buy a package of three or four and keep it in the freezer. I pull one out as needed for these beans.*

### COWBOY BEANS
### Yield: 8 to 10 servings

1 pound package dried red beans
1 pound package dried pinto beans
1 ham bone, ham hock, or several pieces of sliced bacon
1 large onion, chopped
2 cloves garlic
1 tablespoon salt, or to taste
½ teaspoon pepper

• Place beans in a colander and run water over them to wash well. Pick out any bad beans or rocks.
• Place the beans in a large soup pot and cover with water. Allow to soak overnight or for several hours.
• Drain off water and refill with fresh water to cover beans at least 1 inch.
• Stir in remaining ingredients, cover, and simmer 1 to 1½ hours, or until beans are tender, adding more water if needed.
• Can be simmered up to 3 hours or until desired thickness.
• Taste for enough salt.

### QUICK COWBOY BEANS
*Serve with corn bread and a tossed salad.*

If you don't have the time for a long-simmering pot of beans, buy both red beans and pintos in cans and heat them together, along with 1 cup frozen chopped onions, 1 teaspoon chopped garlic, and salt and pepper to taste. Simmer 15 to 20 minutes until onions are cooked.

Cook up a big pot of these beans, and you will have several meals under your belt! They are great served with flour tortillas and a tossed salad. You can add them to a taco salad. Put leftover beans in a skillet and mash them as you reheat them. They become refried beans for burritos or tacos. In doubt? Add chilies!

For additional flavor, add 1 can (4 ounces) chopped green chilies during the last 30 minutes of cooking time.

## SLOW-COOKED FRESH GREEN BEANS LIKE GRANDMA'S
### Yield: 4 servings

1 piece bacon, cut into small pieces
½ cup chopped onion
2 pounds fresh green beans, washed and trimmed
2 teaspoons salt, or to taste
½ teaspoon pepper

- In a large saucepan, fry bacon until crisp.
- Add onion. Cook and stir until tender, about 1 minute.
- Add green beans, salt, and pepper. Cover with lid.
- Simmer about 1 hour.

*Slow cooking may seem like overcooking, but green beans turn out meltingly tender and remind us of Sunday dinner at Grandma's. When you cook them this way, you can also add in some chopped onion, garlic, mushrooms, or sliced almonds at the beginning of the cooking time.*

KIDS USUALLY LOVE FRESH GREEN BEANS. WHEN BUYING FRESH, PICK THROUGH THEM AND TAKE ONLY THE THINNEST, MOST TENDER ONES. CUT OFF BOTH ENDS OF EACH BEAN. THIS IS EASIEST IF YOU HOLD SEVERAL TOGETHER ON A CUTTING BOARD, LINE UP THE ENDS, AND SLICE THEM TOGETHER, THEN CUT THEM INTO PIECES. IF THEY ARE REALLY TENDER, YOU CAN STIR-FRY THEM IN A SKILLET WITH A LITTLE VEGETABLE OIL. KEEP THE HEAT MEDIUM-HIGH. COOK AND STIR ABOUT 5 TO 8 MINUTES OR UNTIL BEANS ARE HOT AND TENDER.

DOUBLE
OVEN DUTY:
*Plan to serve roasted
broccoli when you are
serving Roasted
Rosemary Potatoes.
You will be
able to cook two
things in the
hot oven.*

## OVEN-ROASTED BROCCOLI
Yield: 4 servings

1 pound broccoli flowerettes, washed and well drained
2 tablespoons olive or vegetable oil
1 teaspoon salt
$\frac{1}{2}$ teaspoon pepper

- Preheat oven to 450°.
- In a large bowl, toss together all ingredients.
- Spread coated broccoli in a single layer on a baking sheet.
- Roast 10 to 12 minutes, turning once until tender and beginning to brown around the edges.

*Low-fat cottage
cheese and cheddar
cheese work great in
this recipe. To save
calories, omit the
butter and spray
the baking dish
with vegetable oil.*

## BROCCOLI AND CHEESE CASSEROLE
Yield: 4 servings

1 egg
1 tablespoon flour
$\frac{1}{3}$ cup cottage cheese
$\frac{1}{2}$ cup grated cheddar cheese
1 package (10 ounces) frozen chopped broccoli
1 tablespoon melted butter

- Preheat oven to 350°.
- Beat together the egg, flour, cottage cheese, and cheddar cheese.
- Stir in broccoli.
- Place melted butter in bottom of an 8-inch square baking dish.
- Pour in broccoli mixture and bake 15 to 20 minutes, or until hot and bubbly.

## GLAZED CARROTS
Yield: 4 to 6 servings

1 pound fresh carrots, peeled and sliced into $\frac{1}{4}$-inch pieces
1 cup orange juice
1 tablespoon cornstarch
$\frac{1}{2}$ cup brown sugar
1 tablespoon butter
Pinch of salt

- Steam carrots until tender. Remove from heat and cover to keep warm.
- Meanwhile, make the glaze. Add the cornstarch to the cold orange juice and stir until all cornstarch is dissolved. Pour into a small saucepan.
- Add butter and salt and bring mixture to a simmer, stirring constantly.
- Keep stirring and allow to simmer for 1 minute.
- Pour over hot carrots and toss to coat well.

## BAKED CORN CASSEROLE
Yield: 6 servings

1 package (12 ounces) corn bread mix
1 cup milk
$\frac{1}{4}$ cup vegetable oil
$\frac{1}{4}$ cup finely chopped onion
1 can ($4\frac{1}{2}$ ounces) chopped green chilies
1 cup frozen corn
1 can (1 pound) creamed corn
1 teaspoon sugar
1 teaspoon salt
$\frac{1}{2}$ teaspoon pepper
2 eggs
$\frac{1}{2}$ cup grated cheddar cheese

- Preheat oven to 375°. Spray a $1\frac{1}{2}$-quart baking dish with vegetable oil.
- Combine all ingredients and stir to mix well.
- Pour into prepared baking dish.
- Bake 20 to 25 minutes or until center is almost firm.

## GRILLED CORN ON THE COB
### Yield: 4 servings
*Great served with grilled chicken, beef, pork, fish, or other vegetables.*

4 ears of fresh corn on the cob
2 tablespoons butter or vegetable oil
½ cup fresh thyme, tarragon, or basil
Salt and pepper to taste

- Prepare a charcoal or gas grill
  to medium-high heat.
- Remove husks and silk from
  the corn.
- Place 1 ear of corn on top of a
  large square of heavy-duty foil.
- Dot corn with ½ tablespoon of butter or oil.
- Arrange ¼ of the herbs around the corn and sprinkle all with salt and pepper.
- Wrap securely in the foil. Place corn on prepared grill, about 4 inches from the heat.
- Roast, turning 3 times, for about 10 minutes on each side.
- Look carefully inside the foil of one piece of corn to see if the corn is hot and has
  turned a deep golden color. This means the corn is done.
- If not done, cook a few more minutes and test again.
- Serve hot off the grill.

### COOKING CORN
### IN THE HUSKS

Soak the corn (in their husks) in water for 30 minutes. Carefully pull the husks back from the corn, leaving them attached at the bottom. Remove the silk. Rub the corn with butter or oil, tuck in the herbs, and sprinkle with salt and pepper. Carefully pull the husks back over the corn and place on the grill. Watch ears of corn carefully as they roast since they will cook faster without the foil covering them.

## CORN WITH CHEESE
## AND GREEN CHILIES
Yield: 4 servings

1 cup grated cheddar cheese
1 package (8 ounces) cream cheese, softened
1 can (6 ounces) chopped green chilies
2 teaspoons chili powder
1 teaspoon cumin
1 teaspoon salt
4 cups frozen corn

• Preheat oven to 375°. Spray a 6-cup baking dish with vegetable oil.
• Beat together remaining ingredients.
• Spoon mixture into prepared baking dish.
• Bake 20 to 25 minutes, or until hot and bubbly.

## COLORFUL CORN AND OKRA
Yield: 6 servings

½ cup frozen chopped onions and bell peppers
1 package (10 ounces) frozen okra
1 can (15 ounces) chopped tomatoes
1 cup frozen corn
1 teaspoon salt, or to taste
½ teaspoon pepper

• Place all ingredients in a saucepan.
• Cover and simmer gently 5 to 10 minutes.

## EASY HASH BROWNS

*Shred frozen new potatoes (thaw slightly first) and fry in a little oil to make hash browns. Canned potatoes are also great fried up for hash browns.*

## LEMONY NEW POTATOES
### Yield: 4 servings

*Frozen new potatoes are wonderful and make these dishes quick and easy.*

2 to 2½ pounds new potatoes
2 teaspoons salt, divided
¼ teaspoon pepper
Zest of one lemon
Juice of one lemon
1 to 2 tablespoons butter

• Scrub potatoes. If they are large, cut into smaller pieces.
• Place in a saucepan with 1 teaspoon salt. Add water until potatoes are barely covered.
• Cover and cook gently for 5 to 8 minutes or until tender.
• Drain. Toss with remaining 1 teaspoon salt, pepper, lemon juice, lemon zest, and butter.

## PARSLEY POTATOES
### Yield: 6 servings

2 dozen small new potatoes, scrubbed and trimmed
4 tablespoons butter
1 shallot, minced
3 teaspoons minced garlic
1 bunch fresh parsley, minced
¾ cup fresh bread crumbs
1 teaspoon salt
½ teaspoon pepper

• Gently boil potatoes until just tender. Drain.
• While potatoes are cooking, prepare the parsley sauce.
• Melt butter in a skillet over medium heat.
• Add the shallot and garlic. Cook 3 minutes.
• Stir in parsley and bread crumbs.
Cook, stirring until bread crumbs are lightly brown, about 10 minutes.
• Stir in salt and pepper. Toss with cooked and drained potatoes.

## CHEESY POTATO CASSEROLE
Yield: 8 servings

6 large baking potatoes, cooked until just barely tender
¼ cup melted butter
1 can (15 ounces) cream of mushroom soup
2 cups sour cream
½ cup chopped green onions
2 tablespoons chopped pimentos, optional
1½ cups grated cheddar cheese

• Preheat oven to 350°. Lightly spray a 9 x 13-inch baking dish with vegetable oil.
• Peel cooked potatoes and grate them into a large bowl.
• Stir in remaining ingredients and spread mixture in prepared baking dish.
• Bake 45 minutes.

*If you want to make this a main dish, add chopped cooked chicken, turkey, or ham to the potatoes along with the sour cream.*

## CHEESY SCALLOPED POTATOES
Yield: 6 servings
*To make Ham and Cheese Scalloped Potatoes, add 1 cup chopped or sliced ham to the layers with the onions.*

6 russet potatoes, peeled and thinly sliced
1 large onion, thinly sliced
6 tablespoons butter
4 cups grated cheddar cheese
1 tablespoon salt
1 teaspoon pepper
2 cups milk

• Preheat oven to 375°. Spray a 9 x 13-inch baking dish with vegetable oil.
• Arrange ⅓ of the sliced potatoes in the bottom of the prepared baking dish.
• Layer ⅓ of the onions. Dot with 2 tablespoons of butter.
Sprinkle a little salt and pepper.
• Repeat layers 2 more times. Pour milk over all.
• Bake 1 hour or until potatoes are tender and casserole is hot and bubbly.

## BACON AND BLUE CHEESE
## STUFFED POTATOES
Yield: 4 to 6 servings

4 large russet potatoes, baked until tender
$\frac{1}{2}$ cup sour cream
$\frac{1}{4}$ cup blue cheese crumbles
$\frac{1}{4}$ cup milk
4 tablespoons butter
1 teaspoon salt
$\frac{1}{2}$ teaspoon pepper
4 slices bacon, cooked and crumbled

• Preheat oven to 400°.
• Slice the potatoes in half and gently scoop out the cooked pulp.
Reserve the potato shells.
• Beat together the cooked potato pulp, sour cream, blue cheese,
milk, butter, salt, and pepper.
• Spoon mixture back into reserved potato shells.
• Place filled shells on a baking sheet and bake for 15 minutes or until hot.
• Sprinkle bacon crumbles on top of each potato.

## ARIZONA POTATOES
Yield: 8 to 10 servings

6 medium potatoes
$\frac{1}{2}$ cup butter, melted
2 cups grated cheddar cheese
3 or 4 green onions, chopped
2 cups sour cream
1 teaspoon salt
$\frac{1}{2}$ teaspoon pepper

• Simmer potatoes in boiling salted water until just tender, about 12 minutes.
• Drain, cover, and refrigerate overnight.
• Preheat oven to 375°. Spray a 9 x 13-inch baking dish with vegetable oil.
• Grate cold potatoes coarsely and combine with remaining ingredients.
• Spread mixture in prepared baking dish.
• Bake 30 minutes or until hot and bubbly.

## GARLIC AND PARMESAN MASHED POTATOES
### Yield: 6 to 8 servings

8 large potatoes
½ cup heavy cream
½ cup whole milk
¼ cup butter (4 tablespoons)
2 cloves garlic, minced
¾ cup shredded Parmesan cheese

• Peel potatoes and cut into large chunks.
• Place potatoes in large saucepan. Cover and cook in 1 inch of boiling salted water for 12 minutes or until fork tender. Drain.
• Return potatoes to saucepan. Heat and stir 1 minute over low heat to dry potatoes.
• In a small saucepan, warm the cream, milk, butter, and garlic until butter melts.
• Mash potatoes with a hand mixer, gradually adding warm cream mixture.
• Mix with masher until fluffy and creamy.
• Stir in Parmesan cheese.

## ROASTED ROSEMARY POTATOES
### Yield: 4 servings

4 large russet potatoes, washed and peeled
2 tablespoons chopped fresh rosemary or 1 tablespoon dried rosemary
4 cloves garlic, minced
¾ cup olive oil
Salt and pepper to taste

• Preheat oven to 450°.
• Cut potatoes into bite-sized pieces.
• On a large baking sheet, toss all ingredients to coat potatoes.
• Bake 20 to 25 minutes or until potatoes are browned and tender.

WHAT'S THE DIFFERENCE BETWEEN SWEET POTATOES AND YAMS? YAMS ARE NOT ACTUALLY POTATOES, BUT STARCHY, UNDERGROUND STEMS OF TROPICAL VINES. IN COOKING, YOU WON'T BE ABLE TO TELL THE DIFFERENCE BETWEEN THE TWO. YOU CAN CHOOSE EITHER FOR ANY RECIPE.

## BAKED SWEET POTATOES
### Yield: 4 servings
*Sweet potatoes are juicy and sugary
and will drip while baking,
so be sure to place them on a baking sheet.*

4 medium-sized sweet potatoes
Butter, salt, and pepper to taste
Maple syrup or brown sugar to taste

- Preheat oven to 375°.
- Scrub potatoes, dry, and place on a baking sheet. Pierce each with the tip of a paring knife.
- Bake 1 hour or until tender when pierced in the center with a paring knife.
- Cut open each baked potato. Fluff the center with a fork.
- Add butter, salt, and pepper. Mix.
- Drizzle on maple syrup, or sprinkle on brown sugar. Mix again with a fork.
- Serve piping hot.

*Kids think these baked sweet potatoes
are a treat since they are sweet and buttery!
You will feel good serving them
since they are full of vitamins!*

## SWEET POTATOES AND APPLES
### Yield: 8 servings

4 large sweet potatoes, baked until tender
3 large cooking apples, peeled and cored
⅓ cup white sugar
½ cup brown sugar
1 teaspoon cinnamon
½ cup butter
1 can (6 ounces) frozen apple juice concentrate, undiluted and thawed

• Preheat oven to 375°. Spray a 2-quart baking dish with vegetable oil.
• Peel baked sweet potatoes and cut into ¼-inch slices.
• Cut apples into ¼-inch slices.
• Mix together white sugar, brown sugar, and cinnamon.
• Layer potato and apple slices in prepared baking dish, sprinkling each layer with sugar mixture and dotting with butter.
• Pour apple juice concentrate over all.
• Bake 35 minutes or until apples are tender, and casserole is hot and bubbly.

*Sweet Potatoes and Apples can be baked up to 2 days ahead. To reheat, remove from refrigerator and allow to sit at room temperature for several hours. If baking cold, increase the baking time by about 10 minutes.*

## SPANISH RICE
### Yield: 6 to 8 servings

2 cups rice, rinsed well and drained
3 cups chicken stock
1 Knorr tomato-flavored bouillon cube
2 tablespoons vegetable oil
1 cup chopped onion
2 garlic cloves, minced
1 teaspoon cumin
2 teaspoons chili powder
1 tablespoon each, salt and pepper

*Rinsing the rice is an important step, since it removes the outer starchy covering that makes cooked rice sticky. If you rinse it well, you will have fabulous, fluffy rice!*

- Heat the chicken stock and bouillon cube until the cube is dissolved.
- In a large saucepan that has a lid, heat the vegetable oil; add onion and garlic, and sauté until onion is tender.
- Add the rice, and sauté until the rice begins to brown.
- Stir in cumin, chili powder, and chicken stock; bring to a boil.
- Cover and simmer 20 minutes. Uncover rice and fluff with a fork.

## PECAN WILD RICE PILAF
### Yield: 4 servings

2 cups chicken stock
3 or 4 green onions, thinly sliced
½ cup wild rice
2 tablespoons chopped parsley
1¾ cups brown rice
Juice and grated zest of 1 orange
½ cup chopped pecans
½ cup dried currants
1 teaspoon salt
½ teaspoon pepper

- In a saucepan, bring broth to a boil.
- Add wild rice to boiling broth. Bring back to a boil.
Cover and simmer 50 minutes or until rice is tender.
- Meanwhile, in another saucepan, bring 3¼ cups water to a boil
and stir in brown rice. Cover and simmer 15 minutes or until tender.
- Combine all cooked rice with remaining ingredients. Toss well.

## CREAMY CHEESE SPINACH
### Yield: 4 servings

2 packages (10 ounces each) frozen chopped spinach, thawed
1 package (3 ounces) cream cheese
2 teaspoons salt
1 teaspoon pepper
2 cups grated cheddar cheese

- Preheat oven to 375°. Spray a 2-quart baking dish with vegetable oil.
- Drain spinach. Place in a colander and press out as much water as possible.
- Stir together the spinach, cream cheese, salt, and pepper.
- Place mixture in baking dish and top with grated cheese.
- Bake 20 minutes or until hot and bubbly.

## BAKED WINTER SQUASH
### Yield: 4 servings
*Winter squash are very hard to peel.*
*Baking them in their skins is the simplest way to cook them.*

2 medium winter squash
2 teaspoons salt
1 teaspoon pepper
4 tablespoons butter
4 tablespoons brown sugar

*What is winter squash? It is all those interesting-looking squash that appear at the grocery store in the fall. Acorn and butternut are the most common, but there are also turban, Hubbard, and buttercup.*

- Preheat oven to 350°.
- Wash squash. Cut each in half. Remove seeds and stringy fibers from the centers.
- Place on a baking sheet.
- Sprinkle each with salt and pepper.
- Place in each cavity 1 tablespoon each of butter and brown sugar.
- Bake 35 to 45 minutes until tender.
- To eat, let each person use a fork or spoon to scoop out bites of the tender, sweet inside, leaving the peelings.

## SQUASH CASSEROLE
Yield: 4 servings

*This is such a pretty casserole.*
*It will make your table look like you are having company.*

1 package (1 pound) frozen yellow
  or zucchini squash
½ cup chopped onion
½ cup chopped bell pepper
1 cup crushed butter crackers
2½ cups grated cheddar cheese, divided
2 eggs
½ cup evaporated milk
1 teaspoon salt
½ teaspoon pepper

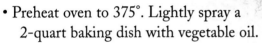

- Preheat oven to 375°. Lightly spray a
  2-quart baking dish with vegetable oil.
- Combine all ingredients, except ½ cup of the
  cheese, in a large bowl and stir with a fork
  to combine well.
- Place in baking dish and bake 25 minutes.
- Quickly pull the baking dish out of the oven.
  Stir casserole if needed and top with remaining ½ cup cheese.
- Bake an additional 5 minutes.

## FRESH TURNIP GREENS
Yield: 4 servings

1 piece bacon, cut into small pieces
½ cup chopped onion (frozen is fine)
2 pounds fresh turnip greens
2 teaspoons salt, or to taste
½ teaspoon pepper

- In a large saucepan, fry bacon until crisp. Drain fat.
- Add onion, and cook another 2 minutes or until tender.
- Add turnip greens and about 1 inch of water along with the salt and pepper.
- Cover and cook about 20 minutes, or until greens are tender.

## BAKED STUFFED TOMATOES
### Yield: 4 servings

4 medium tomatoes
1 package (10 ounces) frozen chopped spinach, thawed
1 package (3 ounces) cream cheese
2 tablespoons pine nuts, optional
2 teaspoons minced garlic
1 teaspoon salt
½ cup grated Parmesan cheese plus extra to top tomatoes

- Preheat oven to 375°. Lightly spray an 8 x 8-inch baking dish with vegetable oil.
- Cut ⅛-inch tops off each tomato. Remove pulp from inside tomatoes.
- Squeeze spinach to remove as much water as possible. Combine with remaining ingredients. (Cream cheese will be chunky.)
- Fill tomato cups and place in prepared baking dish.
- Sprinkle tops with Parmesan cheese.
- Bake 20 minutes or until hot.

*What to do with the leftover tomato pulp? Add it to a can of vegetable soup, a tossed salad, or stir into prepared spaghetti sauce.*

## BUTTERY TURNIPS
### Yield: 4 servings
*Fresh raw turnips are delicious when peeled and sliced very thin.*
*Let your kids shake on some salt or dip them in onion dip, lemon juice, or ranch dressing.*

1½ pounds turnips
2 teaspoons salt, or to taste
Pepper to taste
2 tablespoons butter

- Peel turnips using a carrot peeler. Cut into bite-sized pieces.
- Place in a saucepan and add about 1 inch of water and the salt.
- Cover and simmer about 5 minutes or until just tender.
- Drain off water and toss turnips with pepper and butter.

## SCALLOPED ZUCCHINI
## AND TOMATOES WITH BASIL CREAM
### Yield: 4 to 6 servings

3 tablespoons butter
2 tablespoons flour
1 cup half-and-half
¼ cup chopped, fresh basil
1 teaspoon chicken stock base
1 teaspoon minced garlic
1 teaspoon salt
½ teaspoon pepper
3 medium zucchini, thinly sliced
6 Roma tomatoes, thinly sliced
1 medium onion, thinly sliced
Salt and pepper to taste
½ cup grated Parmesan cheese

- Preheat oven to 350°. Spray a 2-quart baking dish with vegetable oil.
- In a skillet over medium heat, stir together the butter and flour. Cook and stir for 2 minutes to cook flour.
- Whisk in the half-and-half, basil, chicken stock base, garlic, salt, and pepper.
- Stir and cook until thickened, about 3 to 4 minutes.
- Remove from heat.
- Layer half the zucchini, tomatoes, and onion in prepared baking dish, seasoning each layer lightly with salt and pepper.
- Sprinkle half the cheese on top.
- Repeat layers, except for cheese.
- Spoon basil cream over all, and top with remaining cheese.
- Bake uncovered for 45 minutes or until golden brown.

## FIRE STATION JALAPENO CHICKEN
Yield: 6 servings

1 large chicken, cut into 8 pieces,
  or 6 chicken breast halves
2 bell peppers, roughly chopped
2 medium onions, roughly chopped
2 cloves garlic or 2 teaspoons chopped garlic
1 can (20 ounces) pineapple chunks, drained
2 cups bottled barbecue sauce
1 tablespoon sliced, pickled jalapenos, or to taste

- Preheat oven to 375°.
- In a large baking dish, combine chicken and remaining
  ingredients.
- Bake 45 minutes or until largest pieces of chicken are
  done.

*This is a great recipe my brother made when he took his turn
cooking at the fire station. We almost named it Too Easy
Jalapeno Chicken because it is so simple to throw together! All
ingredients can be kept on hand, if you use frozen, chopped bell
peppers and onions. If you use frozen chicken breasts, allow
more baking time to allow the frozen meat to cook through.*

CHOPPED GARLIC IS AVAILABLE IN JARS FROM THE GROCERY STORE. IT SAVES TIME PEELING AND CHOPPING! AFTER OPENING THE JAR, IT WILL KEEP ABOUT 3 WEEKS IN THE REFRIGERATOR.

## HEARTY AND WONDERFUL CHICKEN AND RICE
Yield: 4 servings

1 cup uncooked rice
1 jar (16 ounces) creamy Alfredo sauce
1 can (4 ounces) sliced mushrooms with juice
1 cup chicken stock
4 chicken breast halves (or your favorite chicken pieces)
1 cup dry white wine
1 envelope dry onion soup mix

- Preheat oven to 350°. Spray a 9 x 13-inch baking dish with vegetable oil.
- Stir together the rice, Alfredo sauce, mushrooms, and chicken stock. Spread in the
  bottom of the baking dish.
- Lay chicken pieces on top and pour the wine over them.
- Sprinkle the dry onion soup mix on top.
- Cover with foil and bake 1½ hours. Don't peek!

## CHICKEN AND DUMPLINGS
### Yield: 6 servings
*Your house will smell divine when you cook
up this dish!*

3 boneless, skinless chicken breast halves, about 1¼ pounds
6 cups water
2 chicken bouillon cubes or the equivalent in chicken base
2 teaspoons salt
1 teaspoon mixed Italian herbs (found in spice department)
2 bay leaves
1 cup frozen mixed peas and carrots
1 prepared piecrust, cut into strips
½ cup flour

*You can add extra flavors such as canned green chilies, a small jar of chopped pimentos, frozen chopped onions and peppers, or even a can of green beans.*

- Slice each chicken piece into 6 or 8 pieces; place all in a large saucepan and cover with the water.
- Place over high heat and bring to a simmer. Skim off the foam.
- Lower the heat to medium-low and stir in the bouillon cubes, salt, herbs, and bay leaves.
- Cover and simmer 30 minutes. Uncover the pot.
- Use a wooden spoon to break up the chicken into bite-sized pieces.
- Add the peas and carrots. Bring mixture to a boil.
- Dip each pastry strip into the flour, coating both sides.
- With the mixture boiling, drop pastry strips, one at a time, into the pot. Do not stir—this will break up the dumplings.
- After all pastry strips are added, allow to simmer 10 minutes or until dumplings are thoroughly cooked.
- Serve in soup bowls.

*Make sure the chicken mixture is boiling when you add the pastry strips. This keeps the dumplings from being tough.*

## CHICKEN DIJON
Yield: 4 servings

4 chicken breast portions
½ cup Dijon mustard
½ cup sour cream
1 cup crushed herb-seasoned stuffing mix

• Preheat oven to 325°.
• In a medium bowl, stir together mustard and sour cream.
• Place crushed stuffing mix in a flat bowl or on a plate.
• Dip chicken breasts into sour cream mixture and roll in stuffing mix.
• Place coated chicken in a greased baking dish.
• Bake 45 minutes or until the largest portion reads 155°
on an instant-read thermometer.

## CHICKEN MARSALA
Yield: 6 servings

6 boneless chicken breast halves
1 stick butter
1 tablespoon vegetable oil
Flour for coating chicken pieces
1 teaspoon salt
½ teaspoon pepper
½ cup chopped onion
¼ cup capers, drained
2 tablespoons lemon juice
¾ cup dry Marsala wine

*Capers are the buds from a certain bush grown in the Mediterranean region. They are pickled in vinegar and are used in many Italian recipes. Marsala is an Italian white wine.*

• Pound chicken pieces until thin.
• Combine flour, salt, and pepper, and coat pounded chicken pieces.
• Melt butter and oil in a large skillet over medium-hot heat.
• Add chicken pieces, a couple at a time, and cook 2 minutes.
Turn pieces and cook another 2 minutes or until lightly browned.
• Add the onions, capers, lemon juice, and wine.
• Cook 5 to 10 minutes or until chicken is done.
• Remove chicken to serving platter and pour sauce over top.

*Bake two chickens at once and put one in the refrigerator for the next day's dinner. This saves baking time and also gives you an instant meal. To reheat the chicken, cut into 8 pieces. Place chicken and any vegetables you cooked in a skillet with lid. Add about ¼ cup water or chicken stock.*

*(I throw in ½ bouillon cube and ¼ cup water.) Cover and simmer 10 minutes or until chicken is hot. If you want to vary the flavors of the two dinners, season one chicken with the herbs and the other with lemon pepper (omitting the original pepper in the recipe).*

# CHICKEN IN A BAG
## Yield: 6 servings

*Instead of a whole chicken, you can use individual pieces of chicken. Bake only 1 hour—smaller pieces cook faster than a whole chicken. This dish also works using thick-cut pork chops. Bake them 1 hour.*

1 whole chicken, about 4 pounds
2 tablespoons vegetable oil
2 tablespoons Italian herbs (premixed in a bottle in spice department)
2 teaspoons salt
1 teaspoon pepper
1 large Reynold's Oven Cooking Bag
2 large carrots, peeled and cut in half
6 small red potatoes, scrubbed but not peeled
1 onion, peeled and sliced
½ cup water
1 tablespoon flour

- Preheat oven to 350°.
- Wash chicken inside and out, removing giblets.
- Rub the outside of the chicken with the oil, and sprinkle with the herbs, salt, and pepper.
- Place the chicken inside the cooking bag.
- Arrange the vegetables around the chicken, and pour the water over the vegetables.
- Sprinkle everything with the flour.
- Close the bag according to package directions and place the filled bag on a baking sheet (to catch any spills).
- Bake 1½ hours.
- Remove from oven. Carefully open the bag. Arrange chicken and vegetables on a serving platter. Pour the juices over everything.

## CHICKEN SPAGHETTI CASSEROLE
Yield: 10 servings

*This recipe has many ingredients and quite a few steps.*
*But the results are worth it—the recipe makes lots and it is delicious!*

3 pounds boneless, skinless chicken breasts
½ cup butter
1 large onion, chopped
4 ribs celery, chopped
2 green bell peppers, chopped
1 pound sliced mushrooms
3 cups chicken stock
1 large can tomato juice
½ cup stuffed green olives
3 tablespoons chili powder
3 teaspoons salt
1 pound dry spaghetti
1 pound processed American cheese, cut into cubes
½ cup dry sherry, optional

• Poach chicken breasts.
• Chop cooked chicken and set aside.
• In a large pan, melt butter and sauté the onion, celery, peppers, and mushrooms.
• Add chicken, chicken broth, tomato juice, olives, chili powder, and salt. Simmer this
   mixture for 30 minutes.
• Preheat oven to 350°.
• Meanwhile, cook the spaghetti in boiling water until tender, about 6 minutes.
• Drain spaghetti and fold into simmering sauce.
• Stir in the cheese and sherry.
• Place in a large baking pan and bake 30 minutes.

## CHICKEN, RICE, AND ARTICHOKE CASSEROLE
Yield: 6 to 8 servings

*You may use frozen vegetables or canned green beans in place of the artichokes.*

2 cups dry rice
2 cups water salted with 1 teaspoon salt
1 tablespoon butter or vegetable oil
½ cup chopped onion
½ cup chopped celery
2 cups White Sauce (recipe below)
1 can (6 ounces) sliced mushrooms with juice
1 cup grated cheddar cheese
3 to 4 chicken breast halves, cooked and cubed
1 package (10 ounces) frozen artichoke quarters

• Lightly spray a 9 x 13-inch baking dish with vegetable oil.
• Place rice and salted water in a covered saucepan and cook until rice is just tender, about 15 minutes. Place in bottom of prepared baking pan.
• Meanwhile, preheat oven to 375°.
• In a large saucepan, melt the butter and cook the onion and celery until tender.
• Stir in remaining ingredients.
• Spread mixture over rice.
• Bake 15 minutes or until hot and bubbly.

---

## WHITE SAUCE
*White sauce is used for binding casseroles and foods.*
*White sauce adds flavor and richness to recipes. This recipe makes 2 cups.*

2 tablespoons butter
2 tablespoons flour
2 cups milk
1 teaspoon salt
½ teaspoon pepper

• Melt butter in a skillet over medium heat.
• Add flour, and stir and cook for 1 minute until all flour is cooked and well saturated with butter.
• Remove from heat and stir in the milk, salt, and pepper. Stir until smooth.
• Return to heat and cook, stirring constantly until mixture comes to a simmer.
• Simmer 1 minute, stirring the whole time.

## INSTANT-READ THERMOMETERS

Once you learn to use one of these, you will wonder what you ever did without it. You will never again have to guess when food is done. Instead of slicing into your meat or poking your finger into a plate of food you are microwaving, simply insert your instant-read thermometer and know in a jiffy if it is ready. Here are some handy temperatures to get you started.

*Meat*
Chicken is done and safe to eat at 155°.

*Beef*
Rare: 120° to 125°.
Medium-rare: 125° to 140°
Medium: 145° to 155°
Well-done: 160°

*Pork:* USDA-recommended heat to assure safety: 160°. Cooking meat to this level of heat will make it overdone and dry. Since the temperature of a roast will continue to rise about 5° after it is removed from the oven, we cook pork to 145° and let it stand for 10 minutes after removing from the heat. You may do this, or you may wish to follow the USDA guide.

*Fish* is done at 145° to 150°.

*Bread* is done at 200°.

*Microwaving:* Heating up food in the microwave can be a great time-saver to everyday cooks. For cooking food the first time, 145° insures safety and doneness. For reheating food, 155° insures you have killed any bacteria that may have invaded the food as it was stored.

*Drinks* like tea and coffee are "hot" at 175°.

## ROASTED ROSEMARY CHICKEN
### Yield: 6 servings

1 large, whole roasting chicken, about 4 pounds
2 teaspoons seasoned salt
½ stick butter, cut into 8 pieces
2 tablespoons chopped garlic
2 tablespoons dried rosemary
   or 4 sprigs fresh rosemary
1 tablespoon vegetable oil
Extra seasoned salt for sprinkling on top

- Preheat oven to 350°.
- Remove giblets from chicken and
  wash the chicken well.
- Use your fingers to gently lift up the
  skin around the breast of the chicken.
- Hold the chicken with the legs up.
  (It helps to rest it on a dishcloth so it
  doesn't slip.) Sprinkle the seasoned salt
  evenly under the skin. (You can spread it
  around with your fingers.)
- Distribute the butter, garlic, and rosemary evenly under the skin.
- Fold the chicken's wings under the neck area and tie the legs together with kitchen
  string.
- Place chicken in a roasting pan and bake for 1¼ hours. Chicken is done when
  instant-read thermometer reads 155° in the thickest part of the meat, or juices
  from this area are clear.
- Allow chicken to rest 10 minutes before carving.

*This is an all-time favorite at our
cooking school. Noncooks love it because it is easy yet looks and tastes
gourmet—like the ones from the French cafés!*

## PARSLEY, SAGE, ROSEMARY, AND THYME-ROASTED CAPON
### Yield: 6 to 8 servings

1 capon, 4½ to 5 pounds
About 4 sprigs fresh parsley
4 to 6 fresh sage leaves or 1 tablespoon dried
2 tablespoons fresh rosemary leaves or 1 tablespoon dried
1 tablespoon fresh thyme leaves or 2 teaspoons dried
1 teaspoon each, salt and pepper
1 clove garlic
1 medium shallot, cut into fourths
¼ cup olive oil
1 cup chicken stock

- Preheat oven to 375°.
- Remove giblets from capon. Wash capon well and pat dry with paper towels.
- In a food processor, combine herbs, salt, pepper, garlic, shallot, and olive oil. Process until creamy. You may also chop with a knife.
- Rub this mixture over the entire bird, inside and out. (This can be done ahead, the capon covered well and refrigerated 1 day.)
- Place capon in a baking dish and pour the chicken stock into the dish.
- Bake 2 to 2½ hours, basting every 15 minutes with the pan juices. Capon is done when an instant-read thermometer reads 155° in the thickest part of the meat or when the juices are clear from the thickest part.
- Allow capon to rest 10 minutes before carving.
- Serve with pan juices drizzled on top.

KALAMATA OLIVES ARE FROM GREECE AND HAVE A VERY DISTINCT AND ROBUST FLAVOR. YOU MAY HAVE TO ASK YOUR GROCER TO GET PITTED ONES AS THEY USUALLY COME WITH PITS. IF YOU DON'T HAVE THEM, SUBSTITUTE COMMON, PITTED BLACK OLIVES. THE FLAVOR WON'T BE AS DISTINCT, BUT THE DISH WILL BE FINE!

## ITALIAN CHICKEN AND PASTA
### Yield: 4 to servings

1 pound angel-hair pasta
2 tablespoons olive oil
1 pound skinless, boneless chicken breasts
Salt and pepper to taste
1 jar (8 ounces) sun-dried tomatoes in oil
1 tablespoon minced garlic
¼ cup fresh basil
1 can (8½ ounces) artichoke hearts, drained and sliced
½ cup pitted kalamata olives, sliced
½ cup chicken stock

- Place a large saucepan of salted water over high heat. When it comes to a boil, add dry pasta, and stir to separate strands. Cook for 3 minutes or until pasta is just tender. Drain immediately.
- Meanwhile, heat olive oil in a large skillet over medium-hot heat.
- Slice chicken breasts into diagonal strips and sprinkle all sides with salt and pepper.
- Add coated chicken pieces to the hot oil and cook on all sides until lightly browned, about 3 or 4 minutes.
- Add dried tomatoes (including the oil), garlic, basil, artichoke hearts, chicken broth, and olives. Bring mixture to a simmer.
- Cook, stirring often, for 10 to 12 minutes.
- Add feta cheese and stir to combine.
- Place the cooked pasta on a large platter and top with chicken mixture.

*Chicken stock from the can is fine and so is stock made from bouillon cubes. Of course, homemade chicken stock is the first choice for taste, and it is also the most economical when you use excess chicken parts you have saved up in the freezer.*

## SKEWERED STEAK KABOBS
### Yield: 6 to 8 servings

2 pounds top round or sirloin steak
¾ cup soy sauce
¼ cup water
1 tablespoon grated ginger
1 clove garlic, minced
8 wooden skewers (12-inch)

- Trim meat of all fat. Cut into 1½-inch pieces.
- Combine soy sauce, water, ginger, and garlic.
- Stir meat into sauce and marinate overnight.
- Prepare charcoal grill. Soak skewers in water for 30 minutes.
- Run meat pieces through skewers, creating 8 kabobs.
- Cook meat over hot coals for 25 minutes, turning several times until meat is cooked to desired doneness.

*For skewered chicken kabobs, substitute chicken breasts for the steak and then follow the same recipe.*

GINGER IS THE ROOT OF A TROPICAL PLANT NATIVE TO CHINA. IT HAS A SPICY, PUNGENT FLAVOR AND AROMA. IT IS SOLD FRESH IN THE PRODUCE DEPARTMENT OF YOUR GROCERY STORE IN CLUMPS CALLED "HANDS." THE HANDS HAVE FINGERLIKE SHAPES AND TAN SKIN. NO NEED TO PEEL GINGER; JUST GRATE THE PIECES ON A SMALL CHEESE GRATER. PULL AWAY ANY LOOSE PEELING OR LARGE STRANDS THAT ACCUMULATE.

## *Great leftover!*

*Grill extra chicken wings and then reheat them for a quick meal the next day. Preheat the oven to 400° and bake them 5 minutes or until hot.*

### GRILLED HONEY-LEMON CHICKEN WINGS
Yield: 4 servings
*Serve with Grilled Corn and Garlicky Toast.*
*These wings are also great broiled.*

16 to 18 meaty chicken wings
1 teaspoon mixed Italian herbs
Juice of 2 lemons, about ⅓ cup
1 tablespoon honey
2 tablespoons bottled barbecue sauce
Dashes of Tabasco sauce, if you want spicy wings
1 teaspoon each, salt and pepper

- Wash and dry the chicken wings and allow to drain on paper towels.
- Place remaining ingredients in a large glass or stainless steel bowl. Mix well.
- Add chicken wings and stir to coat well. Cover and marinate in the refrigerator 30 minutes or up to 6 hours.
- Prepare a charcoal or gas grill to medium-hot heat.
- Remove wings from the marinade and grill, turning to brown both sides, 15 to 20 minutes, or until crispy and cooked completely.

## SWEET AND SOUR CHICKEN
### Yield: 4 to 6 servings

1 can (8 ounces) pineapple chunks
1 cup pineapple juice
1 cup cider vinegar
1 cup chicken stock
¼ cup soy sauce
1½ cups sugar
4 fully cooked chicken breast
  halves, cubed
3 cups frozen Oriental-style
  vegetable mix
4 tablespoons cornstarch

• In a Dutch oven, combine
  pineapple chunks, juice, vinegar,
  stock, soy sauce, and 1¼ cups of the sugar.
• Bring to a simmer, stirring to dissolve the sugar.
• Add the chicken and frozen vegetables. Cover and simmer 15 minutes.
• Stir together the remaining ¼ cup sugar and the cornstarch.
• Stir this into the chicken mixture, cooking and stirring until mixture thickens and
  turns clear.
• Serve over cooked rice or Chinese noodles.

*Cornstarch thickens this sauce and gives a lovely clear and glossy look.
Stir it into ¼ cup of the sugar before adding. This keeps the starch from making
little lumps in the liquid. The sugar separates individual starch molecules and keeps
them from attaching to each other to form the lumps!*

## SPECIAL FAMILY MEMORIES

A friend of mine raised nine children on a limited budget but with unlimited special effects! On Friday night, her kids knew they could always invite a friend over because Dad always cooked hamburgers on the grill and always cooked extras. This became such a fun tradition in their family that as they grew up, the children invited their dates over for hamburgers before going out for the evening. You might want to start a "Friday-Night Special" at your house!

- During the year, look for interesting paper plates, napkins, and cups on sale. Use them for your family cookouts. You can use all the various patterns—they don't have to match!
- You can also use pie pans for plates, bandanas for napkins, and canning jars to hold drinks.
- If you serve canned drinks, ice them down in a bucket or metal tub. Tie a bandana on the handle of the bucket.
- Keep a red-checked plastic tablecloth for this special night. It will make your table look festive. It is easy to wipe clean and store in the cabinet.
- For a quick centerpiece, use a canning jar to hold greenery or flowers. Tie a piece of raffia around the jar, making a bow.

*"Entertaining is an expansive gesture and demands an expansive state of mind in charge."*
Martha Stewart

# Friday-Night Hamburger Bash

## PERFECTLY GRILLED HAMBURGERS

Measure ½ to ¾ cup of ground beef. With your hands, shape the meat into a hamburger patty. Use your fingers to make a small hole in the very center of each. When cooking, this hole will allow heat to penetrate the center of the burger and help it to cook evenly. When done, the hole will not be noticed.

## DAD'S REALLY GOOD "SECRET SAUCE"

For a great hamburger sauce, stir together 1 cup ketchup, ½ cup mayonnaise, ¼ cup drained pickle relish, and a little grated onion.

## SET UP FOR A GREAT HAMBURGER BUFFET!
*Use large platters and arrange in a colorful pattern the following:*

Shredded lettuce or lettuce leaves
Thinly sliced onions
Sliced pickles
Sliced fresh mushrooms
Slices of ripe tomato
Grated cheddar cheese, slices of American cheese, and/or
    blue cheese crumbles
Blue Cheese Dressing

## SIDE DISHES

Spiced Almond Tea or Mint Tea
Gazpacho
Corn and Black Bean Salad
Sweet Marinated Slaw
Mom's Potato Salad
Barbecue Baked Beans
Cowboy Beans
Chili Cheese Corn

## EASY SKILLET BARBECUED CHICKEN

Place desired number of chicken pieces in a skillet and cover with barbecue sauce. Cover and simmer 25 minutes, or until chicken is done.

> *This sauce can also be used for grilling meat and fish, on hamburgers or turkey sandwiches. Great added to baked beans.*

### BARBECUE SAUCE
Yield: 2½ cups

1 cup ketchup
½ cup cider vinegar
1 teaspoon sugar
1 teaspoon chili powder
½ teaspoon salt
¼ teaspoon pepper
1½ cups water
3 ribs celery, finely chopped
½ cup finely chopped onion
2 cloves garlic
¼ cup vegetable oil
¼ cup Worcestershire sauce
1 teaspoon paprika

- Combine all ingredients in a large saucepan and bring to a simmer on medium heat.
- Simmer, uncovered, 15 to 20 minutes.
- Store, tightly covered, in the refrigerator up to 2 months.

## NEW ENGLAND BARBECUE BEEF
Yield: enough for 24 sandwiches!
*Great leftover! Keeps 4 days in the refrigerator or 2 months in the freezer.*

4-pound chuck roast, cooked until very tender
9 cups thinly shredded green cabbage
2 cups ketchup
2 tablespoons lemon juice
2 tablespoons Dijon mustard
$\frac{3}{4}$ cup Worcestershire sauce
1 tablespoon salt
1$\frac{1}{2}$ cups beef broth

• Remove all fat from cooked roast and shred the meat.
• Combine all ingredients in a large Dutch oven. Cover and simmer 1 hour.
• Serve on hamburger buns or on top of mashed potatoes or rice.

*The shredded cabbage in this recipe cooks down and creates a delicious flavor and nice consistency. After it is cooked, you won't be able to tell it is cabbage.*

## VEGETABLE BEEF
Yield: 6 servings

$\frac{3}{4}$ to 1 pound stewing beef
1 large onion, chopped
1 bell pepper, chopped
1 teaspoon minced garlic
1 can (28 ounces) diced tomatoes
1 package (10 ounces) frozen mixed vegetables
$\frac{1}{2}$ cup dry rice
Salt and pepper to taste

• Place stewing beef in a Dutch oven and cover with water.
• Cover and cook 1 hour.
• Add onion, pepper, and garlic. Cook another hour.
• Stir in tomatoes, vegetables, and rice.
• Cook 30 minutes or until vegetables are cooked.
• Taste, and add salt and pepper as needed.

CHICKEN
STROGANOFF
IS ALSO A GREAT
FAMILY DISH.

SUBSTITUTE
CHICKEN STRIPS
FOR THE BEEF.
IN STEP 5,
SIMMER ONLY
20 MINUTES OR
UNTIL CHICKEN
IS TENDER.

## BEEF STROGANOFF

2 tablespoons vegetable oil
2 tablespoons butter
1½ pounds sirloin steak, trimmed of fat
1 large onion, chopped
1 pound fresh mushrooms, sliced
2 cups beef broth
2 teaspoons paprika
1 teaspoon salt
½ teaspoon pepper
2 cups sour cream
2 tablespoons flour

- Heat oil and butter in a large Dutch skillet or sauté pan.
- Cut round steak into thin strips, about 2 to 3 inches long.
- Add meat to heated oil, and brown well on all sides.
- Add onions and mushrooms. Cook 2 minutes.
- Add beef broth, paprika, salt, and pepper. Cover and simmer 30 to 45 minutes or until beef is tender.
- Stir together the sour cream and flour. Add to meat mixture.
- Stir until sauce thickens, but do not let the sauce boil.
- Serve over rice, pasta, or noodles.

## AUNT JAN'S TAMALE PIE
Yield: 8 servings

1 pound ground beef
1 cup chopped onion
1 cup chopped bell pepper
½ cup chopped cilantro
2 cups tomato sauce
1½ cups frozen corn
½ cup sliced black olives
2 teaspoons minced garlic
1 tablespoon sugar
2 teaspoons salt
2 teaspoons chili powder

• In a large skillet, cook and stir the ground beef, onion, and bell pepper
until the onions are tender, about 5 minutes.
• Stir remaining ingredients into meat mixture and simmer 15 minutes.
• Spoon mixture into a 2-quart casserole dish. Top with Cornmeal Crust
(recipe below). Bake 40 minutes or until bubbling hot and crust is golden.

## CORNMEAL CRUST

2 cups cold water
¾ cup cornmeal
1 teaspoon salt
1 tablespoon butter or vegetable oil

• Place all ingredients in a saucepan and cook gently,
stirring constantly until thick and bubbly.
*(Mixture should be thick but spreadable. If too thick, stir in a little water.)*

*Great leftovers!*

*After cooking, meat loaf keeps 4 days in the refrigerator or 2 months in the freezer. Double the recipe and have extra for sandwiches the next day.*

*You can also freeze the meat before cooking. Make up several loaves and freeze before baking. Allow to defrost and then bake as usual.*

## MOM'S SHORTCUT MEAT LOAF
### Yield: 4 servings

1 pound ground beef
1 envelope onion soup mix
½ cup tomato sauce
¼ cup ketchup

- Preheat oven to 350°. Spray a 9 x 13-inch baking pan with nonstick coating.
- Mix together ground beef, onion soup mix, and tomato sauce. Shape into a loaf in the baking pan.
- Spread ketchup on top of meat loaf.
- Bake 1 hour or until internal temperature is 155°.

*"It is hard to judge if one's own mother was a good cook. Hers is the first food we eat and there is nothing to compare it to, and there is so much love around it."*
Federico Fellini

## BEEF AND NOODLE CASSEROLE
### Yield: 6 servings

*Serve with tossed salad and buttered corn. To make ahead, assemble the casserole, cover, and refrigerate up to 3 days. Bake as usual.*

1 package (12 ounces) thin egg noodles
1 pound ground beef
1 cup chopped onion
1 bell pepper, chopped
1 teaspoon minced garlic
1 can (2 ounces) diced tomatoes with juice
1 can (6 ounces) tomato paste
1 teaspoon salt
½ teaspoon pepper
1 cup grated cheddar cheese or
    4 slices American processed cheese

- Preheat oven to 375°. Spray a 2-quart
  baking dish with vegetable oil.
- Cook noodles according to package directions. Drain.
- Meanwhile, in a large skillet, cook meat, onion,
  chopped pepper, and garlic until meat is done.
- Stir in cooked noodles, tomatoes, tomato paste, salt, and pepper.
- Spoon mixture into prepared baking dish and cover with cheese.
- Bake 20 minutes or until hot and bubbly.

*Take this frozen casserole on a family ski trip.*
*It will defrost during the car trip to the mountains.*
*When you get there, it is ready to pop in the oven*
*while you unpack the car!*

# Basic Italian Pastas

*Pasta Primer: Italian pastas come in three basic groups:*
  *1. ribbons and strands*
  *2. shapes*
  *3. tubes*

## RIBBONS AND STRANDS

Thin strands are good with light sauces; thicker strands are better for heavier sauces. Ribbons can be layered for lasagna and other casseroles, or stuffed to create ravioli and tortellini.

  Spaghetti: medium-sized strands
  Capellini: angel-hair pasta (thin strands)
  Fettuccine: flat ribbons, medium width
  Lasagna: thickest flat ribbons
  Linguine: flat spaghetti

## SHAPES. . .

hold sauces well and give good texture in casseroles.

  Conchiglie: shells
  Farfalle: bow ties
  Fusilli: corkscrews
  Orzo: small, rice-shaped
  Rotelle: wagon wheels

## TUBES. . .

are good for meat sauces and casseroles. Large tubes are great for filling.

  Manicotti: large tubes
  Penne: tiny tubes
  Rigatoni: pencil-sized tubes
  Spiral: macaroni, curved tubes
  Ziti: thin straight tubes

# BAKED PASTA WITH SPINACH, CHEESE, AND TOMATOES
## Yield: 6 servings

8 ounces pasta, such as fusilli or farfalle

3 tablespoons olive oil, divided use

2 teaspoons salt, divided use

2 packages (10 ounces each) frozen chopped spinach, thawed

2 teaspoons minced garlic

½ cup finely chopped onion or shallot

1 egg

1 cup ricotta or cottage cheese

1 cup Parmesan cheese

¼ teaspoon pepper

2 cans (14 ounces each) chopped tomatoes, with juice

½ teaspoon dried rosemary, crushed

½ teaspoon dried basil

½ teaspoon oregano

2 cups grated mozzarella cheese


• Preheat oven to 375°. Lightly spray a 9 x 13-inch baking dish with vegetable oil.

• Cook pasta according to package directions.

• Drain cooked pasta. Sprinkle with 1 tablespoon olive oil and 1 teaspoon salt.

• Place spinach in a colander and squeeze out as much water as possible.

• Place drained spinach in a bowl and stir in the garlic, onion, egg, ricotta cheese, Parmesan cheese, pepper, and remaining 1 teaspoon salt. Use a fork to mix well.

• Spread the spinach mixture evenly in the prepared baking dish.

• Spread the pasta in an even layer over the spinach.

• Spread the canned tomatoes with their juice over the pasta layer.

• Toss the mozzarella cheese together with the 2 remaining tablespoons olive oil, the rosemary, basil, and oregano. Sprinkle over the tomato layer.

• Place a loose piece of foil over the top and bake 20 minutes. Remove foil and bake another 5 minutes.

TO CRUSH THE CRACKERS, USE A FOOD PROCESSOR AND PULSE UNTIL THE CRACKERS LOOK LIKE CORNMEAL. OR BREAK UP THE CRACKERS, PLACE THEM ON A CUTTING BOARD, AND USE A ROLLING PIN OR HEAVY SMOOTH DRINKING GLASS TO ROLL AND CRUSH.

## CRISPY FISH NUGGETS FROM THE OVEN
### Yield: 4 servings

4 tablespoons butter
¾ cup crushed butter crackers
¼ cup grated Parmesan cheese
1 teaspoon dried Italian herb blend
1 teaspoon salt
½ teaspoon pepper
2 pounds white fish fillets such as cod or sole

- Preheat oven to 375°. Melt butter and pour into bottom of 9 x 13-inch baking dish.
- In a flat pan, such as a pie pan, stir together the crackers, Parmesan cheese, herbs, salt, and pepper.
- Cut the fish into serving pieces.
- Dip the fish, one piece at a time, first into the melted butter in the baking dish, then in the cracker mixture, and return it to the buttered baking dish.
- Bake coated fish for 15 to 20 minutes or until flaky.
- Serve with bottled red cocktail sauce, tartar sauce, or lemon wedges.

## QUICK COCKTAIL SAUCE

If you don't have any bottled sauce, you can make one in a snap. Stir together ½ cup mayonnaise, ¼ cup ketchup, 2 tablespoons pickle relish, and 1 tablespoon lemon juice.

## JUDIE'S EASY CHEESY QUICHE
Yield: one 9-inch pie to serve 4 to 6
*You can add just about anything to this quiche mix: chopped ham, turkey,*
*drained vegetables, or chopped green chilies.*

4 cups grated cheese, such as cheddar,
Swiss, or a combination
4 to 5 eggs
9-inch unbaked piecrust

• Preheat oven to 350°.
• Stir together cheese and eggs. Mixture should be thick, like cooked oatmeal.
If it is too thick, add another egg.
• Pour into piecrust and bake 25 minutes or until knife
inserted in center comes out clean.

*This quiche can be put together and frozen. Fill the pie shell and then care-*
*fully set in the freezer. When frozen, wrap well and return to freezer.*
*To prepare, first allow frozen quiche to thaw in the refrigerator overnight*
*or all day. Then preheat the oven and bake as usual.*

## GREEN CHILI AND CHEESE FRITTATA
Yield: one 9-inch pie to serve 4 to 6

2 cups grated Monterey Jack cheese
2 cups grated cheddar cheese
1 can (3 ounces) chopped green chilies
1 can (12 ounces) evaporated milk
2 eggs
1 tablespoon flour

• Preheat oven to 350°. Spray a 9-inch pie pan with vegetable oil.
• Combine all ingredients and stir well.
• Pour into prepared pan.
• Bake 1 hour.

## BACON CHEDDAR PIE
Yield: one 9-inch pie

4 eggs
¾ cup half-and-half
5 slices bacon, cooked crisp and crumbled
2 tablespoons Dijon mustard
2½ cups grated cheddar cheese
9-inch unbaked piecrust

• Preheat oven to 350°.
• Beat together the eggs, half-and-half, bacon, mustard, and cheese.
• Pour mixture into the piecrust.
• Bake 40 minutes or until set in the center.

---

## TOMATO BASIL PIE
Yield: 4 large servings

*Crimping the piecrust gives your pie a finished look and helps the crust to have an even shape around the edges. There are no rules, so make up your own pattern, or copy what you remember your mom or grandmother doing.*

1 ready-made piecrust, found in the refrigerator section of your grocery store
3 cups grated mozzarella cheese
½ cup fresh basil leaves, found in the produce section of your grocery store
3 to 4 medium tomatoes, sliced ¼-inch thick
2 tablespoons olive oil or vegetable oil
6 pieces bacon, fried crisp and crumbled

• Preheat oven to 375°.
• Line a 9-inch pie pan with the piecrust and crimp the edges.
• Prick the crust all over with a fork and bake for 8 minutes.
• Remove from oven and spread the cheese in the bottom.
• Layer the fresh basil leaves over the cheese.
• Layer the tomatoes over the cheese, overlapping the edges slightly and covering the entire top of the pie.
• Sprinkle with salt and pepper. Drizzle with oil.
• Bake 35 minutes or until tomatoes begin to brown.
• Remove from oven. Sprinkle with bacon and serve.

## ARTICHOKE AND SPINACH FRITTATA
### Yield: 6 servings

*To make this a meat meal, stir in ½ to 1 cup chopped
or sliced ham or smoked turkey.*

*A frittata looks
like a quiche without
a crust. The filling
is baked directly
in the pie pan.*

1 jar (6 ounces) marinated artichokes
1 cup chopped onion
1 teaspoon minced garlic
4 eggs
1 package (10 ounces) frozen chopped spinach, thawed
1 cup Parmesan cheese
½ teaspoon oregano
1 teaspoon salt
½ teaspoon pepper

• Preheat oven to 350°. Spray a 9-inch pie pan with vegetable oil.
• Drain oil from artichokes into a small skillet. Add onion and garlic. Cook until
   onion is tender.
• In a mixing bowl, beat eggs until foamy.
• Dice the artichokes and add to the eggs, along with cooked onion and remaining
   ingredients. Stir well.
• Pour into prepared pie pan and bake 25 minutes.

*This frittata can be served warm
or at room temperature.
It makes a great hors d'oeuvre.
Bake in a 9-inch square pan.
When cool, cut into bite-sized squares.*

THIS RECIPE
DOUBLES, TRIPLES,
OR EVEN
QUADRUPLES
VERY WELL.
WHEN DOUBLING
A RECIPE, DON'T
DOUBLE THE
PEPPER SINCE
PEPPER SEEMS TO
PERMEATE FOODS
AS IT COOKS.
IF YOU QUADRU-
PLE THE RECIPE,
ONLY DOUBLE
THE PEPPER.

## VEGETABLE QUICHE
### Yield: one 9-inch pie to serve 6

9-inch prebaked piecrust
1 tablespoon cooking oil
1 small zucchini, chopped
1 small yellow squash, chopped
$\frac{1}{4}$ cup chopped onion
$\frac{1}{4}$ cup chopped green bell pepper
$\frac{1}{4}$ cup chopped red bell pepper
2 eggs
$\frac{1}{2}$ teaspoon salt
$\frac{1}{4}$ teaspoon pepper
1 cup half-and-half
1 cup shredded cheddar cheese

- Preheat oven to 350°.
- Heat the oil in a large pan and sauté the zucchini, yellow squash, onion, and bell peppers until all vegetables are crisp-tender, about 10 minutes.
- Drain liquid from skillet but keep the cooked vegetables.
- Add remaining ingredients and stir to mix well.
- Pour into prebaked piecrust.
- Bake until set, about 20 minutes. (Cover crust with foil if it begins to get too brown.)

CHAPTER FOUR

*Company's Coming*

# Company's Coming!

*The best* advice you could ever hear for having company is "Prepare ahead!" You don't want to be doing a lot of preparation on the day of your event. Look for recipes and dishes that can be made one to two days before, or even made ahead and frozen. I've learned over the years not to assume, "Oh, I can do that on the day of my party." Unexpected things will always come up that need your attention. It would be better to sit around bored, waiting for your company, than to be tired and frazzled when they arrive.

The second best advice would be to focus on honoring and pleasing your company rather than demonstrating the wonderful things you can do. This mind-set will take the pressure away from having to perform—and you can laugh when things don't go as planned. And I'll bet you will choose easier and less complicated food to serve. If I can share any insight from years of entertaining, it is that fellowship and fun are the important ingredients of a good time together. The food is a catalyst.

The first time I cooked for friends after we were married, the food tasted just awful to me! Two reasons: 1. I wasn't used to cooking, and it really wasn't very tasty! and 2. Your own cooking never seems to taste as good when you are first starting out. But I soon developed a couple of "company dinners" that seemed to turn out well. I served these over and over. Gradually my repertoire grew, and I became very relaxed whenever I entertained. So hang in there, and before you know it, having company will not be the big stress it used to be—if you can get your kids to pick up their mess!

I always like to read about the importance of food during biblical gatherings. I feel we were created with nutritional, emotional, and spiritual needs for which food was given to us. What a gift! To taste, see, feel, smell, and hear food. As God created, I can imagine how He enjoyed putting together His idea of food! Enjoying food together is a theme as old as time.

Take your mind off of trying to impress. Think of making good memories for your children and your guests. Plan ahead. Cook ahead. You go, Girl!

*"Entertaining involves expanding a private world to include others. It calls for an extrovert's heart and an introvert's soul."*
Martha Stewart

# Survival Pantry

### DRY PANTRY:

Flour
Sugar, white and brown
Pecans
Bread, croutons, hamburger buns
Coconut
Crushed pineapple
Black olives, pickles, relish
Canned crabmeat
Oil, vegetable and olive
Red wine vinegar, cider vinegar
Dijon mustard, molasses
Worcestershire sauce
Spices: sage, thyme, cumin, chili powder,
    dill weed, Beau Monde seasoning,
    parsley flakes, bay leaves
Pasta shells
Apple juice
Ginger ale, club soda
Peppermint candies
Chocolate cookies

### REFRIGERATOR:

Butter, milk, eggs
Mayonnaise
Sour cream
Yeast
Anchovy paste in tube
Minced garlic
Sun-dried tomatoes
Bacon
Cheese: cheddar, mozzarella, goat,
    Parmesan

### FREEZER:

Packaged pork tenders
Eye of round roast
Ground beef
Lemonade, pineapple juice
Prepared bread dough
Artichoke hearts
Peppermint ice cream
Whipped topping

### FRESH FRUITS AND VEGETABLES:

Onions
Potatoes
Celery
Bell pepper
Green onions
Parsley
Fresh basil
Lettuce: romaine, leafy green, field greens

# Company Menus

## SUNDAY DINNER

Stuffed Pork Tenderloin with Apple Pecan Stuffing,
Caesar Salad, Angel Biscuits, Pineapple Coconut Cake

## OPEN HOUSE FOR FRIENDS AND FAMILY

Party Punch, coffee, Crab Dip Divine with corn chips,
Bread bowl Dill Dip and various sliced vegetables for dipping,
Braided Bread with Mozzarella, Bacon Dates, small sandwiches with
Pimento Cheese spread, Cheddar Cheese and Pecan Ball with crackers

## COZY FIRESIDE SUPPER

Crab and Artichoke Casserole, tossed salad, Cheese Toast,
Quick Fruit Crisp

## BACKYARD NEIGHBORHOOD PARTY

Hamburger Bash, Strawberry Cake

## SPECIAL NIGHT WITH GRANDMA AND GRANDPA
*(Or lookin' good for your mother-in-law!)*

Eye of Round Roast, Potatoes Cordon Bleu, Garlicky Toasts,
Frozen Peppermint Pie

## HOT CRANBERRY PUNCH
### Yield: ½ gallon
*This punch can be served cold. When served cold, add ginger ale to taste.*

½ cup brown sugar
4 cups water
2 tablespoons lemon juice
½ teaspoon ground cinnamon
½ teaspoon allspice
½ teaspoon cloves
¼ teaspoon nutmeg
2 cans (16 ounces each) jellied cranberry sauce
4 cups unsweetened pineapple juice

• Combine all ingredients in a large soup pot.
• Heat and stir until sugar is dissolved and mixture is smooth and hot.

---

## MINT TEA
### Yield: Approximately 1 gallon
*As a rule of thumb, 1 gallon of punch will serve 15 guests.*

3 cups sugar
1½ cups bottled lemon juice
8 tea bags
½ cup mint leaves

• Place sugar and lemon juice in a saucepan and bring to a simmer,
stirring to dissolve sugar. Turn off heat.
• Add 8 tea bags and mint leaves. Cover and steep for 20 minutes.
• Strain mixture. Add water to make 1 gallon.

## FRUIT SLUSH PUNCH
Yield: 2½ gallons

8 cups water
4 cups sugar
1 can (48 ounces) pineapple juice
1 can (6 ounces) orange juice, undiluted
1 can (6 ounces) lemonade, undiluted
Juice of 2 lemons
4 bananas, mashed with a fork

• Combine all ingredients and freeze in empty milk cartons or freezer containers.
• To serve, let sit at room temperature for 20 minutes.
• Combine with 1½ gallons ginger ale.

*If you are serving this in a punch bowl, you can float small scoops of vanilla ice cream in the punch. As the ice cream melts, it adds a creamy richness.*

## COCOA MOCHA PUNCH
Yield: 2 gallons

1 cup sugar
1-quart boiling water
1 container (16 ounces) chocolate syrup
1 jar (2 ounces) instant coffee

• Add sugar to boiling water and stir to dissolve.
• Stir in chocolate syrup and coffee.
• Pour mixture into a gallon container and finish filling with cold water.
• Refrigerate until ready to serve.
• To serve: Stir well.
• Mix ½ mixture with ½ cup cold milk in punch bowl or pitcher.

*Make this ahead through step 2. (It is easier to store before you add the water.) When ready to serve, start at step 3 and use cold water.*

## RASPBERRY PUNCH
### Yield: 3 gallons

3 quarts raspberry fruit punch
*(Use frozen juice concentrate and follow directions
on container.)*
3 quarts cranberry juice
2 quarts grapefruit juice
3 bottles (1 liter each) ginger ale

• Mix all together and chill.
• Serve over ice in a punch bowl or from a pitcher.

---

## PARTY PUNCH
### Yield: 7 quarts

4 cans (6 ounces each) frozen lemonade, undiluted
4 cans (6 ounces each) frozen pineapple juice concentrate,
undiluted
6 cups water
3 bottles (1 liter each) ginger ale
1 bottle (1 liter) club soda

• Combine first 3 ingredients and mix well; chill.
• To serve, add remaining ingredients and pour over ice in
a punch bowl or pitcher.

## *Having a huge party?*

Here are measurements
for making Raspberry
Punch for 150 guests!
(You can cut it in half
for 75!)

15 quarts raspberry
fruit punch
(10 large frozen
cans)
15 quarts cranberry
juice (10 large
frozen cans)
10 quarts grapefruit
juice (7 frozen
large cans)
15 bottles (1 liter each)
ginger ale

*Tip*

SALSA IS WONDERFUL TO HAVE ON HAND. SERVE IT ON OMELETTES, SCRAMBLED EGGS, WITH FLOUR OR CORN TORTILLAS, ON SALADS—THE IDEAS ARE END-LESS. PUT THIS SALSA IN A 1-QUART CANNING JAR, AND STORE IN THE REFRIGERATOR FOR UP TO 3 WEEKS.

*The following two recipes double well for a crowd.*

### MACHO SALSA
Yield: 1 quart of dip

1 can (28 ounces) chopped tomatoes
1 can (3½ ounces) chopped green chilies
1 jar (3 ounces) chopped pimentos
1 bell pepper, finely chopped
1 bunch green onions, finely chopped
¼ cup finely chopped cilantro
2 teaspoons minced garlic
Salt and pepper to taste

• Combine all ingredients in a nonaluminum bowl.
• Cover and chill several hours to combine flavors.
• Serve with corn chips for dipping.

*We like to serve Texas Caviar on New Year's Day since we observe the Southern tradition of eating black-eyed peas on the first day of the new year. Sometimes we forget about the chips and eat it using a fork and bowl!*

### TEXAS CAVIAR
Yield: 1 quart

3 cans (16 ounces each) black-eyed peas, drained
1 cup chopped bell pepper
¾ cup chopped onion
¼ cup chopped jalapenos, or to taste
1 can (3 ounces) chopped green chilies
2 teaspoons minced garlic
1 cup Italian salad dressing
¼ cup picante sauce or salsa
Salt and pepper to taste

• Combine all ingredients.
• Refrigerate at least 8 hours and up to 3 days.
• Serve with corn chips.

## CHEESY BEAN DIP
### Yield: 6 servings as an hors d'oeuvre
*Everyone loves this dip!*
*Make it ahead and reheat as needed.*

1 can (15 ounces) chili soup, undiluted
1 can (15 ounces) cheddar cheese soup, undiluted
1 can (3 ounces) chopped green chilies
1 pound grated Monterey Jack cheese

- In a saucepan, stir together all ingredients.
- Heat very carefully over low heat, stirring often.
  Heat 8 to 10 minutes or until hot and bubbly.
- Serve with corn chips.

*This is another recipe I have made for at least thirty years. I've had to change the soups a few times as soup makers discontinue some varieties and add others.*

*Basically, it is one can of some type of bean/chili soup and one can of cheese soup. Cheddar cheese could be used in place of Monterey Jack cheese.*

## SPICY CHILI DIP
### Yield: 2 quarts
*If you like things spicy, add a few drops of Tabasco sauce.*

1 pound ground beef
1 large onion, chopped
2 cans (6 ounces) spicy tomato juice
$\frac{1}{2}$ cup canned garbanzo beans
$\frac{1}{2}$ cup raisins
$\frac{1}{2}$ cup black olives, sliced
$\frac{1}{4}$ cup bottled barbecue sauce
1 tablespoon Worcestershire sauce
1 tablespoon salt
1 teaspoon dried thyme
$\frac{1}{2}$ teaspoon dried marjoram
$\frac{1}{2}$ teaspoon pepper

- In a large pot, cook and stir ground beef and onion until
  meat is browned. Drain off juices.
- Add remaining ingredients and simmer 20 minutes.
- Serve hot with corn chips.

TO MAKE AHEAD, COMBINE ALL INGREDIENTS AND PLACE IN BAKING DISH. WRAP AND REFRIGERATE UP TO 3 DAYS. TO HEAT, LET DIP SIT AT ROOM TEMPERATURE DURING THE DAY WHILE YOU ARE PREPARING OTHER THINGS. BAKE IN PREHEATED OVEN AS DIRECTED. IF YOU TAKE IT DIRECTLY FROM THE REFRIGERATOR, ALLOW A FEW EXTRA MINUTES OF BAKING TIME.

## CRAB DIP DIVINE
### Yield: 2 quarts

*This recipe can be made using shrimp, scallops, lobster, or a combination of seafood instead of crabmeat.*

1-quart mayonnaise
8 ounces cheddar cheese, grated (2 cups)
½ cup sliced ripe olives
2 teaspoons cumin
1 tablespoon chili powder
½ cup prepared picante sauce
1 bunch green onion, finely sliced
1 can (6 ounces) crabmeat

- Preheat oven to 350°.
- Combine all ingredients and place in prepared baking dish.
- Bake 12 to 15 minutes or until just hot and bubbly. (Don't overbake or the cheese will become oily.)
- Serve with corn chips or crackers.

## TEXAS CRAB GRASS
### Yield: 4 cups to serve 8 to 10

½ cup butter
1 cup finely chopped onion
1 package (12 ounces) frozen chopped spinach, thawed and drained
1 cup grated Parmesan cheese
1 package (8 ounces) cream cheese

- Heat butter in a skillet and cook onion until tender.
- Stir in remaining ingredients and cook until hot.
- Place in a chafing dish and serve with crackers.

## CRAB BALLS FOR A PARTY
Yield: 2 dozen balls

1 can crabmeat
1 egg
1 cup tomato juice
1 cup finely crushed cracker crumbs
⅛ teaspoon ground red pepper
12 pieces bacon, cut in half to make 24 pieces

- Preheat oven to 350°. Line a baking sheet with parchment paper or spray with vegetable oil.
- Stir together all ingredients except bacon.
- Form mixture into 24 to 30 balls the size of walnuts.
- Wrap each ball with a bacon slice, and place on prepared baking sheet, bacon seam down.
- Bake 25 minutes, turning once to brown all sides.

## BACON DATES
Yield: 24 pieces

12 pieces bacon, each cut in half
24 dates

- Preheat oven to 350°.
- Place bacon halves on a cookie sheet and bake 10 to 15 minutes or until bacon is beginning to cook and curl.
- Cool bacon pieces slightly until easy to handle.
- Wrap one piece around each date, securing with a toothpick.
- Return to oven and bake until bacon is crisp, 5 to 8 minutes.

## CHEDDAR CHEESE AND PECAN BALL
### Yield: 2½ cups cheese spread

1 pound sharp cheddar cheese, grated
¼ cup butter, at room temperature
3 tablespoons grated onion
1 tablespoon grated bell pepper
2 tablespoons Worcestershire sauce
1½ cups chopped pecans

- Place cheese, butter, grated onion, bell pepper, and Worcestershire sauce in a mixer bowl. Beat until smooth.
- Use a rubber spatula and your hands to roll the cheese into a ball.
- Place the chopped pecans on a large piece of plastic wrap, and roll the ball around until all surfaces are completely covered. You might need to lift the plastic wrap and press the pecans into the cheese.
- If time permits, refrigerate until well chilled.
- Serve with crackers or thin slices of dense French bread.

*This is a recipe I've had in my little recipe box since I was a newlywed! I've made it many times. It has been a faithful "whip up" when I need to serve a last-minute snack. Everyone loves cheese, and a cheese ball is a quick and easy treat when unexpected company arrives. If you wish, you can roll the cheese ball in chopped walnuts, chopped parsley, or plain dry paprika.*

## PUFF PASTRY BUTTERFLIES
## WITH HONEY MUSTARD AND PROSCUITTO
### Yield: 3 dozen pastries

1 sheet prepared puff pastry
    (sheets measure 18 x 11 inches)
3 tablespoons honey mustard
¾ cup grated Parmesan cheese
2 ounces paper-thin slices proscuitto
1 egg, beaten with 1 tablespoon water

- Preheat oven to 400°. Line 2 cookie sheets with parchment paper or spray with vegetable oil.
- Unwrap the puff pastry, place it on a work surface, and spread evenly with the mustard.
- Sprinkle cheese evenly over the mustard, and layer on the proscuitto.
- Starting at one long edge, roll up the puff pastry jelly-roll style to the middle of the dough.
- Repeat with the other side, making two rolls that meet in the center.
- Brush the edges where the dough meets with a little of the egg mixture, to seal the edges together.
- Turn the roll over with the smooth side up, and use a serrated knife to cut the roll crosswise into ½-inch slices.
- Place the slices on prepared cookie sheet and brush the tops with the egg mixture.
- Bake 8 to 10 minutes or until puffed and lightly golden brown.
- Serve warm or at room temperature.

**Tip**

PUFF PASTRY BUTTERFLIES ARE ALSO CALLED ELEPHANT EARS OR PALMIERS. INSTEAD OF THE SAVORY FILLING OF CHEESE AND PROSCUITTO, YOU CAN MAKE THE PASTRIES SWEET. TO MAKE SUGAR AND CINNAMON ELEPHANT EARS, SPRINKLE THE FLAT PUFF PASTRY WITH A MIXTURE OF 3 TABLE-SPOONS SUGAR AND 1 TEASPOON CINNAMON. ROLL THE PASTRY AND BAKE AS DIRECTED.

*Prepare through step 8. Freeze on top of parchment or wax paper on a cookie sheet. When frozen, wrap with plastic wrap and then foil. May be frozen up to 2 weeks ahead. To serve, allow to defrost and bake as directed.*

## BRAIDED BREAD WITH MOZZARELLA, BASIL, AND SUN-DRIED TOMATOES
### Yield: 1 braided loaf

1 loaf prepared frozen bread dough, defrosted
1 cup grated mozzarella cheese
$\frac{1}{2}$ cup fresh basil leaves
$\frac{1}{2}$ cup chopped sun-dried tomatoes
1 egg lightly beaten with 1 tablespoon water to make egg wash

- Preheat oven to 350°. Spray a baking sheet with oil or line with parchment paper.
- On a floured surface, roll bread dough into a rectangle, about 12 x 15 inches.
- Sprinkle mozzarella cheese down the center length of the rectangle, leaving a 2-inch border on either side.
- Top cheese with basil leaves and sun-dried tomatoes.
- Along each long edge, use kitchen scissors or a pastry cutter to cut a 2-inch border into $\frac{1}{2}$-inch strips, stopping before you get to the filling.
- Starting at one end, pull one strip over to cover filling.
- Pull the strip from opposite side over filling and crossing over first strip.
- Repeat with all strips, creating a braid. Pinch the ends together to seal the roll.
- Brush entire roll with egg wash.
- Bake 15 to 20 minutes or until golden brown.

*Other fillings for braided bread:*

*Thinly sliced ham and cheese*
*Blue cheese*
*Pepperoni and pizza sauce*
*Sautéed peppers and onions with sausages*
*Brie and pecans*

## DILL DIP FOR VEGETABLES OR CHIPS
### Yield: 2 cups dip

1 cup sour cream
1 cup mayonnaise (low-fat is fine)
1 tablespoon grated onion
1 teaspoon dried dill weed
1 teaspoon Beau Monde seasoning
1 teaspoon dried parsley flakes

- Stir together all ingredients.
- Refrigerate at least 2 hours to chill well and let the flavors develop.

---

## SUN-DRIED TOMATO DIP
### Yield: about 2½ cups

1 package (8 ounces) cream cheese (low-fat is fine)
¼ cup sun-dried tomatoes in oil, drained
½ cup sour cream (low-fat is fine)
½ cup mayonnaise (low-fat is fine)
Juice of one lemon, about 2 tablespoons
1 teaspoon Beau Monde or other seasoned salt
2 green onions, finely chopped

- Place cream cheese and tomatoes in a food processor and process until tomatoes are finely chopped.
- Add sour cream, mayonnaise, lemon juice, and Beau Monde. Pulse the machine a few times until mixture is well mixed.
- Stir in chopped green onions.

## MEDITERRANEAN OLIVE-TOMATO SPREAD

Follow the recipe for Sun-Dried Tomato Dip, adding ¼ cup chopped Italian and/or Greek olives. In a pinch, you can use common black olives.

## BASIC FORMULA FOR QUICK DIPS!

*Need a quick savory snack for unexpected company? If you have sour cream and mayonnaise in your pantries, you are halfway there!*

*The ratio of one-to-one sour cream and mayonnaise is a great way to start a dip, enhanced by whatever goodies you have in your refrigerator or pantry. Try adding dry taco seasoning to taste.*

*Once, I grated red bell pepper into this dill dip, and it was fabulous! Add finely chopped celery, and you have a nice crunch! Chop some artichokes from the can, and stir in ½ cup Parmesan cheese. You eventually will hit on a blend that everyone goes crazy over. Ta-da! You have your own signature dip!*

## BRUSCHETTA WITH TOMATOES
### Yield: 8 servings

½ cup extra-virgin olive oil
4 to 6 cloves roasted garlic or
   3 teaspoons minced fresh garlic
6 to 8 ripe tomatoes, chopped, or
   1½ cups chopped, sun-dried tomatoes
1 large shallot, finely chopped or
   2 green onions, chopped
3 large fresh basil leaves, chopped,
   or 1 tablespoon dried basil
¼ cup chopped Kalamata or other
   black imported olives
1 tablespoon lemon juice
1 teaspoon salt
1 teaspoon pepper
1 loaf crusty Italian, peasant,
   or other dense bread

- Place olive oil and garlic in a small bowl.
  Mash the garlic with a fork to release flavor into the oil. Set aside.
- In a medium bowl, combine the tomatoes, shallot, basil, olives, lemon juice, salt, and
  pepper. Set aside.
- Cut bread into ½-inch slices and toast them on both sides under the broiler or on a
  grill.
- Brush one side of each piece of toast with the garlic and olive oil mixture.
- Drizzle the remaining olive oil over the tomato mixture and stir well.
- Arrange the toast on individual plates or on a serving platter, and top each with the
  tomato mixture.
- Serve immediately.

*Roasted garlic (see page 159) is wonderful on bruschetta, the Italian toasted
bread with interesting toppings. This is an incredibly easy hors d'oeuvre
and one everyone always loves. Sometimes we eat bruschetta as a light supper.*

## ROASTED GARLIC

Whole heads of soft, roasted garlic are a lavish garnish for roasted and grilled meats. Roast a whole head for each person. To eat, use a fork and knife to mash out the soft garlic, leaving the peeling, and spread it on the meat or on bread. Individual roasted cloves are fabulous in cooking. Use in place of fresh garlic for a more subtle and delicate flavor. Or offer on a platter with meats, vegetables, or bread.

*To roast whole heads:* Use a serrated knife to trim off ¼ inch from the tops of the heads of garlic (not from the root end), making a flat surface. Stand trimmed garlic heads, root side down and flat side up, in a small baking dish. Drizzle with olive oil, about 1 tablespoon per head of garlic. Roast in preheated, 350° oven 15 to 18 minutes or until soft and beginning to brown.

*To roast individual cloves:* Separate cloves and place in a small, heavy skillet over medium heat on top of the stove. Add ¼ inch of olive oil. Cook slowly, stirring often, 10 to 12 minutes or until cloves are soft and beginning to brown.

## GOAT CHEESE AND ROASTED GARLIC
### Yield: about 2 dozen servings

6 ounces mild goat cheese
4 dozen garlic cloves, roasted
4 dozen crackers or small slices of sourdough bread

• Place cheese in the center of a serving platter and surround with garlic cloves.
• Offer a cheese knife in the cheese.
• Serve with crackers or bread.

*These cookies will keep in the freezer up to 2 months. Make sure they are wrapped well to prevent freezer burn. Put them in freezer bags or plastic freezer containers.*

## PECAN CHEESE COOKIES
### Yield: about 2 dozen cookies

1 stick butter, softened
½ pound grated cheddar cheese
2 cups flour
½ teaspoon salt
24 pecan halves

- Preheat oven to 350°. Lightly spray a baking sheet with vegetable oil.
- Beat together the cheddar cheese and butter until smooth.
- Beat in flour and salt.
- Drop by teaspoon onto prepared baking sheet.
- Press a pecan half onto the top of each cookie.
- Bake 18 to 20 minutes or until just beginning to brown.

## BLUE CHEESE COOKIES
### Yield: about 1½ dozen cookies

1 stick butter, at room temperature
½ cup blue cheese crumbles
1 cup flour
¼ teaspoon salt
18 pecan halves (optional)

- Preheat oven to 350°. Line a cookie sheet with parchment paper or spray with vegetable oil.
- Beat together the butter and cheese until creamy and well combined.
- Add flour and salt, and mix well.
- Drop by teaspoon onto prepared baking sheet.
- Top each cookie with a pecan piece, if desired.
- Bake 18 to 20 minutes or until lightly browned.

## TOMATO AND ARTICHOKE SALAD
## WITH BLUE CHEESE DRESSING
### Yield: 6 servings

8 ounces blue cheese (divided use)
1½ cups mayonnaise
1½ cups sour cream
2 teaspoons Worcestershire sauce
2 teaspoons minced garlic
1 cup buttermilk
6 medium red and ripe tomatoes
Salt and pepper to taste
1 can artichoke hearts (Look for a can that contains
    6 hearts.)
Juice of 2 or 3 lemons
6 lettuce leaves (leafy green, red-tipped, or butter lettuce)
Parsley for garnishing

- Blend 4 ounces of the blue cheese with the mayonnaise
  and sour cream until smooth. (Use a fork to mash the
  cheese.)
- Stir in Worcestershire sauce, garlic, and buttermilk.
- Meanwhile, cut ¼-inch tops off each tomato.
- Use a paring knife to cut center of each tomato away
  from the sides. Use a spoon to scoop out the pulp. Set
  aside pulp.
- Salt and pepper the insides of each tomato.
- Drain artichokes and generously drizzle lemon juice over
  and inside each one. (This will take away any canned
  flavor.)
- Place one artichoke heart inside each tomato cup.
- Chop reserved pulp and fill in tomato cups around the
  artichoke hearts. (Salad can be prepared ahead of time
  up to this point. Refrigerate tomato cups until time to
  assemble salad.)
- Place one lettuce leaf on each of 6 salad plates and top
  with a tomato cup.
- Spoon blue cheese dressing over the tomato cup, covering
  the artichoke heart and tomato chunks.
- Garnish each with a sprig of parsley or other herb.

*Make Ahead*

*Prepare Blue Cheese
Dressing (steps 1 and 2)
up to 3 days ahead.
Store in an airtight
container in the
refrigerator.*

*The day before, carve the
tomatoes. Place on a
plate, cover with plastic
wrap, and refrigerate.
Place the artichoke hearts
in a small bowl and
drizzle with lemon.
Cover and refrigerate.
Wash the lettuce leaves
and store in a plastic bag.*

*The morning of serving,
fill the tomato cups,
wrap, and refrigerate.
Construct salads just
before serving.*

*Make Ahead*

*Prepare Balsamic Maple Vinaigrette 2 to 3 days ahead. Cover tightly and store in the refrigerator.*

*Prepare Sugared Pecans the day ahead and store in zip-fastener bag or other airtight container.*

*Crumble goat cheese the day before serving. For easy crumbling, let cheese sit in freezer for 30 minutes before crumbling with a fork. Store in a zip bag.*

*Fry the bacon the morning before serving, and keep drained on paper towels at room temperature.*

*Toss the salad (step 1) just before guests arrive (up to 45 minutes before serving). Cover and refrigerate. Toss in the dressing and pecans just before serving.*

## FIELD GREENS WITH BACON, SUGARED PECANS, AND GOAT CHEESE
### Yield: 6 servings

8 to 10 cups baby field greens or torn leaf lettuce
6 to 8 pieces bacon, fried crisp and crumbled
$\frac{1}{2}$ cup crumbled goat cheese
1 recipe Balsamic Maple Vinaigrette
1 recipe Sugared Pecans (below)

• In a large bowl, toss together field greens, bacon, and goat cheese.
• Drizzle on salad dressing and toss to coat evenly.
• Add Sugared Pecans and toss again.

## SUGARED PECANS

$\frac{1}{4}$ cup packed brown sugar
2 tablespoons water
1 cup pecan halves

• Place brown sugar and water in a heavy skillet and cook over medium heat, stirring until sugar is dissolved.
• Add pecans and cook, stirring constantly until all water evaporates, about 5 minutes.
• Spread pecans on a baking sheet until cooled and dry.
• Break apart nuts that are stuck together.
• Store in an airtight container.

## FANCY SHRIMP SALAD IN TOMATO CUPS
### Yield: 6 servings

*This salad can be served as a main course or as a first course for a fancy meal. If used as a first course, the recipe will serve 12. You can cut each tomato in half, making smaller cups.*

6 medium tomatoes
1 cup sour cream
½ cup mayonnaise
1 tablespoon ketchup
1 tablespoon horseradish
1 tablespoon grated onion
1 tablespoon lemon juice
1 teaspoon Worcestershire sauce
1 teaspoon each, salt and pepper
2 tablespoons chopped fresh dill
1½ pounds large shrimp, cooked, peeled, and chilled
2 stalks celery, chopped
½ cup slivered almonds
6 good lettuce leaves
6 slices fresh lemon
6 small sprigs fresh dill

- Cut about ⅛-inch top off each tomato.
- Use a spoon to scoop out the inside pulp.
- Sprinkle insides lightly with salt and pepper. Turn upside down on a plate to drain. Cover and refrigerate until ready to serve.
- In a large bowl, combine sour cream, mayonnaise, ketchup, horseradish, onion, lemon juice, Worcestershire sauce, salt, pepper, and dill. Stir well.
- Fold in shrimp, celery, and almonds.
- To serve, place a lettuce leaf on each plate. Place a tomato cup on each and fill with shrimp mixture.
- Divide remaining shrimp mixture among the 6 plates, placing it on the lettuce leaves. Place a slice of lemon and dill on each plate as a garnish.

*Make Ahead*

*Prepare the dressing (steps 1–3) the morning of the dinner. Wash and dry the lettuce in the morning. Store in plastic bag in refrigerator. Construct salad just before serving.*

*Grated Onion— One great way to get the extra flavor of onion without the crunch is to grate the onion on a metal grater. This also gets lots of onion juice and makes things taste good!*

BUY ANCHOVY
PASTE IN A TUBE,
WHICH ALLOWS
EASY MEASURING.
KEEP UNUSED
PORTION IN THE
REFRIGERATOR.

## CAESAR SALAD
### Yield: 6 servings

1 egg
3 tablespoons red wine vinegar
1 tablespoon Dijon mustard
1 tablespoon anchovy paste (optional)
Juice of 1 lemon (about 2 tablespoons juice)
1 teaspoon minced garlic
1 teaspoon salt
$\frac{1}{2}$ teaspoon pepper
$\frac{3}{4}$ cup olive oil
$\frac{1}{4}$ cup vegetable oil
1 head romaine or leafy-green lettuce, washed and torn
   into bite-sized pieces
1 cup grated Parmesan cheese
3 cups croutons

- In a large salad bowl, whisk together the egg, vinegar,
  mustard, anchovy paste, lemon juice, garlic, salt, and
  pepper.
- In a small bowl, combine olive oil and vegetable oil.
- Drizzle oils into egg mixture in a slow steady stream,
  whisking constantly to combine ingredients.
- Add torn lettuce. Toss to coat well.
- Add Parmesan cheese and croutons. Toss again.

## HEAVENLY YEAST ROLLS
### Yield: 3 dozen rolls

½ cup warm water (not over 110°)
2 packages dry yeast
1 teaspoon sugar
1 cup warm milk
1½ cups melted butter (divided use)
¼ cup sugar
3 eggs
1 teaspoon salt
4½ cups flour

• Place the water in a mixer bowl. Sprinkle on the yeast and sugar; activate yeast.
• Stir in milk, ½ cup of the melted butter, sugar, eggs, and salt. Mix well.
• Add flour and beat well.
• Knead, either with a dough hook or by hand until smooth and very elastic.
• Cover and let rise until double, about 45 minutes.
• Stir down dough and turn onto flour surface. Knead several times.
• Roll out to about 1-inch thickness. Cut out rolls with a 2-inch biscuit cutter.
• Pour ½ cup of the remaining melted butter into a 9 x 13-inch baking dish.
• Place rolls in baking pan, turning over once to coat tops with butter.
• Let rise until double, about 30 minutes.
• Preheat oven to 350°.
• Bake rolls 15 to 20 minutes or until lightly golden brown.

*The morning of your dinner, measure out all ingredients. Place milk and eggs together in a covered bowl in the refrigerator. Prepare baking pan also. Just before baking, mix up batter.*

## COMPANY CORN BREAD
### Yield: 9 x 13-inch pan or 12 large pieces
*This fabulous corn bread is very sweet and has the consistency of cake.*

$\frac{1}{2}$ cup cornmeal
$2\frac{1}{2}$ cups biscuit baking mix
1 cup sugar
$\frac{1}{2}$ teaspoon baking powder
$\frac{1}{2}$ teaspoon ground nutmeg
1 cup milk
3 eggs
$\frac{1}{2}$ cup butter, melted but not hot

• Preheat oven to 350°. Spray a 9 x 13-inch baking pan with vegetable oil.
• In a large bowl, stir together the cornmeal, biscuit mix, sugar, baking powder, and nutmeg.
• Add milk, eggs, and melted butter. Stir or whisk until smooth. A few lumps of biscuit mix may remain.
• Pour into prepared pan.
• Bake 25 minutes or until golden brown and center springs back when touched.

## CRAB AND ARTICHOKE CASSEROLE
### Yield: 4 servings

*This is a perfect recipe to use frozen chopped onions and bell peppers. Add directly from the package—they will defrost during cooking.*

2 tablespoons butter
2 tablespoons flour
¼ teaspoon pepper
1 teaspoon salt
2 cups milk
1 cup dry pasta shells, cooked until just tender
1 package frozen artichokes, cut in halves
½ cup chopped onion or shallots
¼ cup chopped green bell pepper
1 can (6 ounces) crabmeat
¾ cup grated cheddar cheese

- Preheat oven to 350°. Lightly butter a 2-quart baking dish.
- Combine all ingredients, except cheddar cheese. Place in prepared baking dish.
- Top with cheddar cheese.
- Cover lightly with foil and bake 20 minutes.
- Remove cover and bake an additional 10 minutes.

## Make Ahead

*The day before, prepare the casserole through step 3. Cover and place in refrigerator. The next day, bake as directed. Serve with a green salad or fruit salad and Angel Biscuits.*

WHEN COOKING SEAFOOD DISHES, SHALLOTS GIVE A MORE ELEGANT FLAVOR THAN ONIONS. FROM THE ONION FAMILY, SHALLOTS HAVE A SUBTLE FLAVOR AND ARE MORE EXPENSIVE TO BUY. THEY ARE KIND OF LIKE THE HIGH-CLASS BRANCH OF THE ONION FAMILY!

*The morning of your dinner, prepare through step 5. Cover and refrigerate. To serve, bake according to directions.*

## SHRIMP SCAMPI
### Yield: 4 servings

2 pounds fresh, uncooked shrimp, peeled
1 cup butter
¼ cup olive oil
1 teaspoon dried, crushed basil
1 teaspoon dried, crushed oregano
1 teaspoon minced garlic
1 teaspoon salt
1 tablespoon chopped fresh parsley
2 tablespoons fresh lemon juice

- Preheat oven to 450°.
- Place shrimp in a flat baking dish.
- In a skillet, melt butter and olive oil.
- Add basil, oregano, garlic, salt, and parsley. Cook until heated through.
- Pour mixture evenly over the shrimp.
- Place shrimp in oven and bake 5 minutes.
- Open the oven door, turn oven to broil, and broil shrimp for another 5 minutes.

## SHRIMP AND LOBSTER CASSEROLE
### Yield: 6 servings
*Serve this elegant casserole with Caesar Salad,*
*steamed broccoli or other green vegetable,*
*and Heavenly Yeast Rolls.*

¾ cup wild rice
1½ cups chicken stock
¼ cup butter or vegetable oil
3 large shallots, chopped
1 cup chopped celery
8 ounces sliced, fresh mushrooms
2 lobster tails, meat removed and cut into bite-sized pieces
1½ pounds cooked, peeled frozen shrimp
2 cans cream of mushroom soup
¼ cup milk
½ cup slivered almonds

- Spray a 2-quart baking dish with vegetable oil. Set aside.
- Place wild rice and chicken stock in a covered saucepan, and simmer 40 to 50 minutes or until rice is tender and has "popped open."
- Meanwhile, heat butter in a skillet. Cook shallots, celery, and mushrooms until shallots are tender, about 5 minutes.
- Stir in lobster meat, shrimp, soup, milk, and cooked rice.
- Place in prepared baking dish. Sprinkle on almonds and bake 30 minutes.

WILD RICE IS THE GRAIN OF A WATER PLANT AND IS ACTUALLY NOT EVEN RELATED TO RICE. THE GRAINS ARE LONG, SLENDER, AND VERY DARK BROWN. THE GRAINS TAKE LONGER TO COOK THAN REGULAR RICE. THE GRAINS STAY SPRINGY AND HAVE A NUTTY FLAVOR. MOST AMERICAN WILD RICE IS GROWN IN MINNESOTA. IT IS USUALLY SOLD IN THE GROCERY STORE IN A 4-OUNCE OR ½-POUND PACKAGE.

## EYE OF ROUND ROAST
### Yield: 6 servings

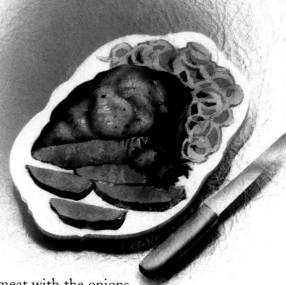

1 cup vinegar
$\frac{1}{2}$ cup molasses
1 large onion, finely chopped
4 or 6 cloves garlic, minced
2 bay leaves
4-pound eye of round beef roast

- In a large bowl, combine vinegar, molasses, onion, garlic, and bay leaves.
- Place roast in the bowl and push down so marinade covers most of the meat.
- Marinate overnight.
- The next day, preheat oven to 325°.
- Remove the roast from the marinade and place in a shallow baking dish.
- Pour marinade over roast, covering the meat with the onions.
- Place a piece of foil loosely over the meat.
- Bake 2 hours, basting with marinade each $\frac{1}{2}$ hour.
- After 2 hours, remove meat to a slicing board.
- Keep juices hot for serving with the meat.
- Slice meat. Serve with juices and horseradish sauce.

## VERY EASY BAKED GAME HENS
### Yield: 4 servings

4 game hens, giblets removed
4 tablespoons vegetable oil
4 tablespoons minced garlic
Salt and pepper, 2 teaspoons each

- Preheat oven to 375°.
- Place hens in a roasting pan.
- Tie legs together with kitchen twine and tuck wings under necks.
- Rub each hen with 1 tablespoon oil, 2 teaspoons garlic, and $\frac{1}{2}$ teaspoon each of salt and pepper.
- Bake 1 hour or until instant-read thermometer reads 155° in the thickest part of the meat.

## CORNISH GAME HENS WITH FRUIT AND NUT STUFFING
### Yield: 4 servings
*Serve with Frozen Fruit Cups*

4 plump Cornish game hens (about 1 pound each)
6 teaspoons minced garlic
2 tablespoons dried oregano
1 teaspoon salt
1 teaspoon pepper
½ cup red wine vinegar
¼ cup olive oil
½ cup each, pitted prunes, dried apricots,
   and pitted green olives
½ cup pecan pieces
¼ cup capers
4 bay leaves
½ cup brown sugar
1 cup apple juice

- Clean hens well under cold running water. Pat dry and place in a large bowl.
- Combine garlic, oregano, salt, pepper, vinegar, olive oil, fruit, pecans, capers, and bay leaves. Pour over the hens.
- Cover bowl and marinate hens overnight in the refrigerator.
- Preheat oven to 350°.
- Arrange hens in a large flat baking dish. Spoon all the marinade over hens.
- Sprinkle evenly with the brown sugar, and pour apple juice around the hens.
- Bake for 1 to 1¼ hours, basting frequently until golden brown, and the internal temperature of the hens is 155°.
- Arrange hens on a serving platter. Surround with baked fruit mixture and drizzle with some of the juices.
- Serve any remaining juices in a sauce bowl.

*Marinate overnight according to directions. The next morning, arrange hens in baking dish. Cover and refrigerate. When ready to bake, simply pop in the oven and bake according to directions.*

## STUFFED PORK TENDERLOIN
Yield: 6 servings

1 package pork tenderloins
  (Each package contains two pieces.)
1 recipe of either Apple Pecan Stuffing or Quick Celery and Onion Stuffing
  (next page)

- Preheat oven to 350°. Spray a baking dish with vegetable oil.
- Flatten and butterfly the tenderloins by making lengthwise cuts into the meat.
- Spread open one piece and mound stuffing along entire surface of meat.
- Lay second tenderloin on top of stuffing and mold into a cylinder.
- Secure with strips of bacon, tucking ends of bacon under meat.
- Place entire stuffed tenderloin in baking dish and surround with extra stuffing.
- Bake 45 minutes to 1 hour or until internal temperature measures 160°.
- Remove from oven and allow to sit 5 minutes before slicing into serving pieces.

## QUICK CELERY AND ONION STUFFING
Yield: 4 servings

2 tablespoons butter
1 medium onion, chopped
2 cups celery, chopped
1 package (8 ounces) Pepperidge Farm Herb Stuffing Mix

• Melt butter in a large skillet. Sauté onion and celery until tender.
• Prepare stuffing according to package directions, adding the onion and celery.

## APPLE PECAN STUFFING
Yield: 8 to 10 servings

½ cup butter
1 medium onion, chopped
1 cup chopped celery
6 cups soft, fresh, white bread crumbs
4 large cooking apples, unpeeled and chopped
2 cups chopped pecans
2 teaspoons dried sage
2 teaspoons dried thyme
2 teaspoons salt, or to taste
1 teaspoon pepper
½ cup chopped parsley
2 large eggs
½ cup apple juice

• Sauté onion and celery in butter until crisp-tender, about 10 minutes.
• Remove from heat and stir in remaining ingredients.
• Stir in more apple juice if mixture is too dry.

A CHICKEN THAT HAS BEEN GROWN LONGER THAN A FRYING CHICKEN, USUALLY 12 TO 18 MONTHS, IS CALLED A STEWING CHICKEN. THE FLAVOR IS THE SAME AS A YOUNGER, SMALLER CHICKEN, BUT IT IS NOT AS TENDER AND USUALLY COSTS LESS. IT NEEDS LONG, MOIST COOKING TO TENDERIZE. YOU CAN ALWAYS SUBSTITUTE A FRYING CHICKEN IN A RECIPE CALLING FOR A STEWING CHICKEN.

## EASY CHICKEN CURRY
### Yield: 6 to 8 servings

*Chicken Curry is easy because it can be completely prepared the day ahead and reheated.*

1 stewing chicken, about 5 pounds (or 3 pounds chicken breasts)
2 tablespoons butter
1½ cups chopped onion
1 bell pepper, chopped
1 teaspoon minced garlic
2 to 3 tablespoons curry powder
1 cup plain yogurt
Salt and pepper to taste
Condiments for serving:
    raisins, coconut, peanuts, chopped scallions, bottled chutney

- Place chicken in a large pot and cover with water.
- Cover with a lid and simmer 30 minutes or until meat is done and easily falls off the bones.
- Drain and save the broth.
- As soon as chicken is cool enough to handle, remove all meat from the bones.
- Meanwhile, heat the butter in a Dutch oven and cook the onions, pepper, and garlic until tender.
- Stir in the chicken, curry powder, and 3 cups reserved chicken broth.
- Cover and simmer for 1 hour, adding broth if mixture gets dry.
- Just before serving, stir in the yogurt.
- Serve from a large serving platter on top of cooked rice.
- Pass condiments to put on top.

*Curry powder is a blend of spices, such as cinnamon, cloves, cumin, ginger, turmeric, pepper, and others that is used in Indian cooking.*

## ELEGANT HAM AND CHICKEN ROLLS IN SHERRY
### Yield: 8 servings

8 boneless chicken breast halves
8 thin slices boiled ham
8 thin slices Swiss cheese
2 eggs
1 cup milk
1 cup flour
1 teaspoon salt
1 can cream of mushroom soup
½ cup water
½ cup dry sherry
¼ cup butter, melted

*The day before, prepare chicken, steps 1–4. Wrap and refrigerate. In the morning, prepare the batter, step 5. Cover and refrigerate. Prepare soup mixture, step 6. Cover and refrigerate. Begin to construct casserole and place in preheated oven 2 hours before serving.*

- Preheat oven to 400°.
- Use a rolling pin or your fist to gently pound and flatten chicken pieces.
- Line each breast with one slice of ham and one slice of cheese.
- Roll up each piece with the ham on the inside. Secure with a toothpick.
- Stir together the eggs, milk, flour, and salt to make a thick batter. Dip each chicken piece in the batter and place in a large baking dish.
- Stir together the soup, water, and sherry. Pour evenly over the chicken pieces.
- Drizzle butter on top.
- Bake 10 minutes at 400°. Lower the oven to 325° and bake an additional 1½ hours.

*Pounding chicken breasts makes them spread out and evenly flat. Use a rolling pin or your fist and gently tap on the thicker places. The meat will easily break down and smooth out.*

*Cook the entire dish the morning of your dinner. Cool, cover, and refrigerate. Reheat over low heat for 25 minutes or until hot and bubbly.*

## COMPANY ROUND STEAK
### Yield: 6 servings
*Serve this dish with rice, mashed potatoes, or buttered noodles.*

2 pounds round steak, cut into serving pieces
2 tablespoons vegetable oil
1 large onion, sliced
1 pound mushrooms, sliced
1/2 cup slivered almonds
1 can (15 ounces) tomato soup, undiluted
1 can (28 ounces) chopped tomatoes with juice

• In a large skillet or sauté pan, heat the oil.
• When hot, add steak pieces and brown on both sides.
• Add remaining ingredients. Cover and simmer 1 1/2 hours.

## TENDERLOIN OF BEEF
### Yield: 8 servings with leftovers
*Serve tenderloin with a tossed salad, Sally Lunn bread, and baked potatoes.*

4 pounds beef tenderloin
1 tablespoon minced garlic
1 tablespoon salt
1 teaspoon pepper

• Preheat oven to 375°.
• Place tenderloin in a baking pan.
• Rub all over with minced garlic. Sprinkle with salt and pepper.
• Uncover and bake 1 hour or until internal temperature is 145° on an instant-read thermometer.
• Remove from oven and let sit 15 minutes before carving and serving.

## POTATOES CORDON BLEU
### Yield: 6 hearty servings

*"So delicious, you just want to roll around in it. . ."*
Julia Watts

2 cups heavy cream
2 cups half-and-half
3 teaspoons chopped garlic
3 teaspoons salt
$\frac{1}{2}$ teaspoon pepper
1 bay leaf
6 large russet potatoes
1 cup sour cream
1 cup grated Swiss cheese or Parmesan cheese

- Place the half-and-half and cream in a large saucepan. Add garlic, salt, pepper, and bay leaf. Heat just below a simmer.
- Peel potatoes and slice into $\frac{1}{8}$-inch slices, dropping them into the heated cream as they are sliced.
- Cook potatoes 10 minutes in the cream.
- Preheat oven to 350°.
- Spread $\frac{1}{2}$ cup of the sour cream in the bottom of a 9 x 13-inch baking dish.
- Spoon hot potatoes, with cooking liquid, evenly over the sour cream.
- Top with remaining $\frac{1}{2}$ cup of sour cream and then sprinkle with the grated cheese.
- Bake potatoes 20 minutes or until hot and bubbly and lightly browned on top.

### Make Ahead

*Prepare through step 7 the day before serving.*
*Cover and refrigerate. To serve, bake as directed.*

**POTATO VARIETIES**

*New potatoes, both red and white, are small, young potatoes that have been harvested early while their skins are still tender. They have waxy flesh and are best for boiling and steaming, but not for baking. They are too wet and sticky for baking. And they become limp when fried.*

*For baking, you need russet potatoes. They are mature potatoes with rough skin and starchy, mealy flesh. They are tender, dry, and fluffy when baked. Good choice for frying. They tend to crumble when boiled, making them fine for mashing or whipping. Purple potatoes are similar to russet.*

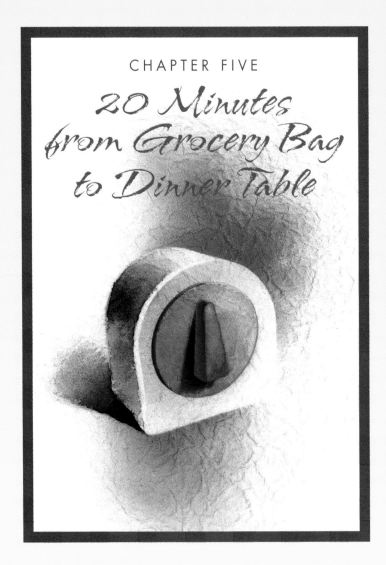

CHAPTER FIVE

# 20 Minutes from Grocery Bag to Dinner Table

# Getting Food on the Table Fast!
### When 20 minutes is all you have.

*I like* to tell noncooks that my goal is not to convince them to *love* to cook. Instead, I like to help them learn to do this part of their job (alas, it is part of our job description as parents) quickly and easily! There are areas we aren't the most fond of in every career. When it comes to parenting, if cooking is not your strong suit, then you are probably great at other parts of parenting! Maybe you like attending sports games, helping with homework, cleaning, and organizing the house. We all have our strong areas. Do these well, and we'll help you out with the cooking.

So many of my cooking-school students constantly ask for menus and recipes that will help them get fun, healthy meals in front of their families—fast! This chapter is devoted to just that.

To cut down on prep time, we have substituted prepared and "convenience" ingredients for the usual ones that take more time to prepare. Frozen chopped onions and peppers are a must for quick dishes. If using canned soup turns you off, substitute bottled Alfredo sauce or make a quick white sauce. Using already-roasted chicken eliminates poaching or roasting time.

Wherever possible, use small, chopped ingredients that cook faster than large pieces. Keep packages of taco seasoning on hand to add flavor to quickly sautéed meat. Since we are cutting down on simmering time, the flavors may not be as defined and mature as in long, slow-cooked dishes, so you need to add extra flavor with more onions, a sprinkle of extra seasoning, and more herbs than usual.

Remember that the most important thing is that as you are sitting down to supper with your children, you are listening to them talk and share. They are getting the message, "You are important enough to me that I have fixed this meal, and I am stopping everything to be with you and enjoy your company!" You are feeding more than their stomachs. You are feeding them emotionally and spiritually as well. Good for you! Great parenting!

# Time-Saving Hints

## MEAT

- Before cooking, cut or slice meats or other ingredients into small pieces to help it cook faster.

## SALAD

- Buy packaged, washed, and trimmed lettuce and other salad ingredients so you can make a salad in a snap.

## VEGETABLES

- Prepared vegetables, such as peeled and trimmed baby carrots, cook fast and make great side dishes.
- Grating onion saves chopping time and allows the onion flavor to spread into the dish quicker. And you don't get big chunks of raw onion.
- Buy chopped garlic in a jar and save time not only chopping, but washing a knife and cutting board.
- Frozen chopped onions and peppers can be added directly from the bag to cooking food. Reseal bag with a twist tie and return to the freezer. Use equal amounts when a recipe measures by the cup. Use this conversion chart to figure the amount to use in a recipe that measures by the individual piece:

  One medium onion equals ¾ cup chopped
  One large onion equals 1 cup chopped
  One medium bell pepper equals ½ cup chopped
  One large bell pepper equals ¾ cup chopped

## PASTA

- Always start water for pasta at the beginning of a recipe calling for cooked pasta. The pasta has time to cook while you put together the sauce.
- Always put a lid on the pot when heating water to boil pasta—it heats twice as fast this way.
- Fresh pasta cooks faster than dried. Angel-hair pasta cooks faster than regular spaghetti.

## HERBS AND SPICES

- Buy mixed Italian herbs in the jar so you don't have to measure each individual herb.

# Survival Pantry

**REFRIGERATOR:**

Butter
Eggs
Milk
Mayonnaise
Sour cream
Chopped garlic
Dijon mustard
Ricotta cheese or cottage cheese
Grated cheese: cheddar, Monterey Jack,
    Parmesan
Cream cheese
Prepared piecrusts

**MEATS:**

Roasted chicken breasts
Sliced ham, bacon
Kielbasa, ground sausage
Ground beef
Chicken pieces
White fish
Salmon fillet

**PRODUCE:**

Green onions
Carrots
Celery
Broccoli flowerettes
Lemons
Spinach
Parsley
Bell peppers
Jicama
Onions
Tomatoes
Granny Smith apples

**FROZEN PANTRY:**

Corn
Peas
New potatoes
Stir-fry vegetable mix
Chopped onions
Chopped bell peppers
Chopped spinach
Cheese ravioli

**DRY PANTRY:**

Pasta, noodles
Corn bread mix
Cornstarch
Rice
Vegetable oil, olive oil
Chopped tomatoes
Tomato sauce
Spaghetti sauce, Alfredo sauce
Salsa and taco sauce
Soy sauce
Worcestershire sauce
Sauerkraut
Green chilies
Black olives
Sliced mushrooms
Chicken stock or bouillon cubes
White wine
Canned tuna or salmon
Corn chips
Saltine crackers
Cream of chicken soup

**HERBS AND SPICES:**

Basil
Cinnamon
Curry powder
Italian herb blend

PLACING A STAINLESS STEEL BOWL OVER A POT OF HOT WATER GIVES JUST ENOUGH HEAT TO WARM THE EGG AND CREAM MIXTURE WITHOUT COOKING IT. BRING A POT OF WATER TO A BOIL AND THEN TURN OFF THE HEAT. THIS SHOULD BE JUST HOT ENOUGH.

## FETTUCCINE ALFREDO
### Serves 4

*Add sliced ham or cooked bacon (¹/₂ to 1 cup)*
*for an even heartier version of Alfredo!*
*For vegetarian, add sautéed bell peppers and onions.*

2 tablespoons butter
1 teaspoon salt
¼ teaspoon pepper
2 eggs
½ cup heavy cream
1 cup Parmesan cheese
1 pound fettuccine

- Bring a large pot of water to a boil.
- Meanwhile, melt the butter in a large stainless steel bowl placed over a pot of hot water.
- Stir in salt, pepper, eggs, heavy cream, and Parmesan cheese. Mix well.
- Boil fettuccine until just tender.
- When pasta is cooked, toss with the sauce, using a little of the pasta cooking water if needed for moisture.

## LINGUINI WITH SPINACH AND BACON

Yield: 4 servings

*Serve this rich dish with tossed salad
and Garlicky Toast.*

6 slices bacon, cut into slivers
12 ounces linguini
1 package (10 ounces) fresh, triple-washed spinach
4 ounces cream cheese (low-fat is fine)
2 tablespoons milk
2 teaspoons dried Italian herbs
1 teaspoon salt
½ teaspoon pepper

- Place bacon slivers in a large skillet over medium-high heat and fry until crisp. Drain fat.
- Meanwhile, bring a large pot of water to a boil for the pasta. Cook pasta until just tender.
- Add the spinach to the cooked bacon. Cover with a lid for a few minutes to wilt the greens.
- Stir in remaining ingredients, and stir until cheese is melted and sauce is smooth.
- Stir in drained pasta.

TO QUICKLY SLICE BACON, PULL THE AMOUNT YOU NEED COLD FROM THE REFRIGERATOR, LEAVING THE PIECES STACKED TOGETHER. PLACE IT ON A CUTTING BOARD AND USE A FRENCH-BLADE KNIFE TO MAKE THIN CUTS ACROSS THE SHORT ENDS, CUTTING ALL PIECES AT ONCE.

## BROILED WHITEFISH
## WITH GARLIC LEMON BUTTER
Yield: 4 servings

*Serve fish with Lemony New Potatoes.*

$\frac{1}{2}$ stick butter, at room temperature
Zest of 1 lemon
3 tablespoons grated onion
2 teaspoons minced garlic
2 tablespoons minced fresh parsley
$\frac{1}{2}$ teaspoon salt
$\frac{1}{4}$ teaspoon pepper
2 pounds whitefish fillets
Juice of 1 lemon

- Preheat oven broiler.
- Meanwhile, use a fork to mash together the butter, lemon zest, onion, garlic, parsley, salt, and pepper.
- Place the fish pieces in a glass baking dish and cover with the lemon juice.
- Divide the butter mixture between the fish pieces and spread evenly with a knife.
- Place the fish 4 to 5 inches from the heat.
- Broil until fish becomes opaque and is flaky in the center. The time will depend on how thick the fish is. Cooking time will be about 10 minutes per 1 inch of thickness of the fish.
- Serve on a platter with cooking juices drizzled over.

*I have made this recipe with many kinds of whitefish—talapica, swordfish, sole—even shrimp and scallops!*

## QUICK CHICKEN CACCIATORE
### Yield: 4 to 6 servings

1 pound rigatoni pasta
1 can (28 ounces) chopped tomatoes with juice
1 tablespoon tomato paste
1/2 cup frozen chopped onions
1/2 cup frozen chopped bell peppers
1 teaspoon minced garlic
1 teaspoon each, dried rosemary and oregano
1 teaspoon salt
1/2 teaspoon pepper
1 roasted chicken from the grocery deli, cut into 8 pieces

- Cook pasta according to package directions.
  While pasta is cooking, prepare the tomato sauce.
- In a Dutch oven or deep skillet with a lid, combine the
  tomatoes, tomato paste, onions, bell pepper, garlic,
  rosemary, oregano, salt, and pepper.
- Cover with a lid and bring to a medium simmer. Simmer
  for 5 minutes.
- Remove lid. Add chicken pieces, pushing them down
  into the sauce.
- Simmer 15 minutes.
- Place hot, cooked pasta on a large serving platter and top
  with chicken mixture.

*Add other interesting ingredients your family likes to this dish,
such as:*
    Canned mushrooms
    Artichoke quarters
    1 cup frozen peas
    Sliced ham or cooked bacon (stir in at the last)
    Canned miniature corn

TOMATO PASTE
CAN BE BOUGHT
IN A SMALL CAN
OR A TUBE. THE
TUBE IS HANDY
WHEN YOU ONLY
NEED A SMALL
AMOUNT.
STORE UNUSED
PORTION IN THE
REFRIGERATOR.

## CHICKEN AND GREEN CHILI STEW
### Yield: 6 servings
*Serve this stew with warm flour tortillas and shredded lettuce
with Mexican Ranch Dressing.*

1 can (28 ounces) chopped tomatoes
$^1/_2$ to $^3/_4$ cup chicken broth
10 to 12 ounces roasted chicken breast, diced
1 cup frozen chopped onions
1 cup frozen chopped bell peppers
2 cloves garlic, chopped
2 cans (4 ounces each) chopped green chilies
4 to 6 frozen new potatoes
1 cup frozen sliced carrots
Salt and pepper to taste

• In a Dutch oven or large deep skillet with a lid, combine all ingredients.
• Cover and simmer 20 minutes, adding more chicken broth if needed.

## CHICKEN CURRY DIVAN
### Yield: 6 to 8 servings
*You can use canned green beans or mixed frozen vegetables in place of broccoli.*

$^1/_2$ pound broccoli, cut into small flowerettes
2 cups cooked, sliced chicken
1 can low-fat cream of chicken soup
1 cup low-fat sour cream
1 cup low-fat mayonnaise
1 tablespoon lemon juice
$^1/_4$ teaspoon curry powder
$^3/_4$ cup grated cheddar cheese

• Preheat oven to 375°.
• Place broccoli in bottom of 9 x 13-inch baking dish and arrange chicken on top.
• Stir together soup, sour cream, mayonnaise, lemon juice, and curry powder.
• Pour mixture over chicken.
• Sprinkle top with cheese.
• Bake 20 minutes or until hot and bubbly.

## CHICKEN AND GREEN CHILI CASSEROLE
Yield: 6 servings

1 can low-fat cream of chicken or cream of mushroom soup
1 soup can of milk
1 medium onion, chopped
1 can (4 ounces) diced green chilies
1 teaspoon salt
$\frac{1}{2}$ teaspoon pepper
12 corn tortillas, torn into pieces
2 cups cooked chopped chicken
2 cups grated cheddar cheese

• Preheat oven to 375°.
• Lightly spray a 2 quart baking dish with vegetable oil.
• Place the soup, milk, onion, chilies, salt, and pepper in a saucepan.
• Heat until hot and bubbly.
• Add corn tortillas and stir until all tortillas are well coated.
• Place half the mixture in the prepared baking dish and cover with half the cheese.
• Repeat layers.
• Bake 20 minutes.

THICKENING WITH CORNSTARCH GIVES SAUCES A SHINY, CLEAR LOOK. YOU MUST FIRST DISSOLVE THE CORNSTARCH IN A LITTLE LIQUID. PUTTING DRY STARCH DIRECTLY INTO A LARGE AMOUNT OF LIQUID WILL CAUSE LUMPS.

## CHICKEN ORIENTAL
### Yield: 6 to 8 servings

2 tablespoons butter or vegetable oil
1 cup chopped onion
1 green pepper, chopped
1½ cups chopped celery
½ pound sliced mushrooms
3 cups cooked chicken, shredded
2¾ cups chicken stock
4 tablespoons cornstarch
1 teaspoon salt
¼ teaspoon pepper
1 tablespoon soy sauce

- Melt butter in a Dutch oven. Add onions and peppers. Cook 2 minutes.
- Add mushrooms, celery, and chicken. Cook, stirring often, for another 6 minutes.
- In a medium bowl, whisk together ¼ cup of the chicken stock and cornstarch. This will make a paste. When the paste is smooth, whisk in remaining broth.
- Stir this mixture into hot chicken mixture and stir vigorously until bubbly and clear.
- Stir in salt, pepper, and soy sauce. Cook another 5 minutes.
- Serve over rice or Chinese noodles.

## CHICKEN STOCK

Homemade chicken stock is wonderful, but canned is also very good. In recipes like this one, canned works great and so do chicken bouillon cubes or chicken base.

Some people say bouillon cubes are too salty. Well, then just don't add as much salt to your recipe. Works great! Hey, when your goal is to get food on the table fast, giving up the flavor of homemade stock or broth is a price you can pay.

## CHILI CHEESE CORN
### Yield: 4 servings

1 cup grated cheddar cheese
1 package (8 ounces) cream cheese, softened
1 can (6 ounces) chopped green chilies
2 teaspoons chili powder
1 teaspoon cumin
1 teaspoon salt
4 cups frozen corn, thawed

- Preheat oven to 375°. Spray a 6-cup baking dish with vegetable oil.
- Beat together cheddar cheese, cream cheese, chilies, chili powder, cumin, and salt. (Cream cheese will be lumpy.)
- Stir in corn.
- Place mixture in prepared baking dish.
- Bake 20 minutes or until hot and bubbly.

TO QUICKLY SOFTEN CREAM CHEESE, REMOVE FROM FOIL WRAPPER. PLACE ON A PIECE OF PLASTIC WRAP, FOLD OVER THE PLASTIC WRAP TO COVER THE CHEESE, AND ZAP IN THE MICROWAVE FOR 20 SECONDS.

## CREAM CHEESE SPINACH
### Yield: 4 servings

2 packages (10 ounces) frozen chopped spinach, thawed
1 packages (3 ounces) cream cheese (low-fat is fine)
2 teaspoons salt
1 teaspoon pepper
2 cups grated cheddar cheese

- Preheat oven to 375°. Spray a 6-cup baking dish with vegetable oil.
- Drain spinach, place in a colander, and press out as much water as possible.
- Stir together the spinach, cream cheese, salt, and pepper. (Cream cheese will be lumpy.)
- Place mixture in baking dish and top with cheese.
- Bake 20 minutes or until hot and bubbly.

## DUCK SOUP!
### Yield: 6 to 8 servings

*There isn't any duck in this soup—it's just VERY easy to make! Serve Duck Soup
with corn chips or a pan of corn bread.*

1 pound ground beef or turkey
1 cup chopped onion
1 package taco seasoning mix
1 package ranch dressing mix, dry
1 can (15 ounces) Mexican-style corn
1 can (15 ounces) chopped Mexican-style tomatoes
1 can (15 ounces) Mexican-style pinto beans
1 can (4 ounces) chopped green chilies
1 cup water

• In a large soup pot, cook and stir ground beef until brown, breaking up pieces as it
  cooks.
• Drain accumulated fat from meat.
• Add remaining ingredients to cooked meat. Simmer 15 to 20 minutes.

## PASTA FAGIOLI
### Yield: 6 large servings

1 can (1 pound) cannelloni or Northern white beans, undrained
1 can (28 ounces) chopped tomatoes
2 cans (15 ounces each) beef broth
1 jar (16 ounces) traditional-style spaghetti sauce
1 cup chopped onion
2 ribs celery, thinly sliced
2 cups dry macaroni
1 teaspoon salt or to taste
$^1/_2$ teaspoon pepper

• Place all ingredients in a large soup pot and cover with a lid.
• Simmer 30 minutes.

## SKILLET FRITTATA
## WITH HAM AND CHEESE
Yield: 4 servings

1 tablespoon vegetable oil
½ cup frozen chopped onions
½ cup diced or sliced ham
1 teaspoon salt
½ teaspoon pepper
5 eggs, beaten together
1 cup grated cheddar cheese

• Heat the oil in a large skillet over high heat. Cook the onion and ham until they begin to get browned.
• Stir salt and pepper into beaten eggs.
• Turn heat to medium-low and add eggs to ham and onion mixture in skillet, stirring to mix well.
• Use a flat spatula to stir, gathering the mixture toward the center of the pan.
• When the eggs begin to set, spread mixture out and top with cheese.
• Turn the heat to low and cover skillet with a lid.
• Allow to cook slowly for 5 minutes or until all eggs are done.

*A skillet frittata is like a large omelette that you don't have to turn in the pan. A baked frittata is like a quiche without a bottom crust. Both are hearty and great for family meals.*

SEEDING TOMATOES REMOVES THE JUICE AND SEEDS AND MAKES LESS LIQUID IN YOUR RECIPE. CUT THE TOMATO IN HALF CROSSWISE; HOLD ONE HALF IN YOUR PALM AND GENTLY SQUEEZE OUT THE SEEDS INTO A BOWL. REPEAT WITH OTHER HALF. THESE SEEDS AND JUICE CAN BE EATEN OR ADDED TO SOUPS OR SALADS.

## FRITTATA WITH SPINACH AND TOMATOES
### Yield: 4 to 6 servings

1 tablespoon vegetable oil

1 cup frozen chopped onions

10 ounces fresh spinach, washed and drained

3 tomatoes, seeded and chopped

4 eggs, beaten together

1 cup milk

1 cup grated Monterey Jack cheese

2 teaspoons dried basil

1 teaspoon salt

$\frac{1}{2}$ teaspoon pepper

$\frac{1}{4}$ cup grated Parmesan cheese

- Heat oil in a large skillet over medium-high heat.
- Add all ingredients except for the Parmesan cheese.
- Cook and stir about 3 minutes.
- Turn heat to medium-low.
- Top mixture with grated Parmesan cheese.
- Cover and cook 10 to 12 minutes or until mixture is just set in the middle.

## GARLICKY TOAST
### Yield: 4 servings

*Keep this garlic butter spread in the refrigerator, tightly wrapped for up to 2 months. Besides Garlicky Toast and bread, it is great on sandwiches, cooked vegetables, and meat. Melt some on meat or vegetables when you are grilling.*

2 tablespoons butter
1 teaspoon chopped garlic, or 1 teaspoon garlic salt,
or ½ teaspoon garlic powder
½ teaspoon salt
4 thick slices of French or sourdough bread

- Preheat oven broiler.
- Blend the butter, garlic, and salt.
- Spread butter mixture on bread slices and place them on a baking sheet.
- Place about 4 inches from broiler heat and toast until golden brown, about 3 minutes.

---

## CHEESE TOAST
### Yield: 4 servings

*In a pinch, you can certainly make cheese toast with any bread you have on hand. Use a mixture of cheeses if you don't have enough of one kind.*

4 slices country-style or sourdough bread
½ cup grated cheese, such as cheddar, Swiss, or Monterey Jack

- Preheat oven broiler.
- Place bread slices on baking sheet.
- Top evenly with cheese.
- Broil 3 to 4 minutes or until cheese is melted and beginning to bubble.

*Assemble this casserole
(through step 5) before
leaving for work.
Cover and refrigerate.
After work, place over a
medium-low stove
burner and simmer
10 to 12 minutes or
until ravioli is done.*

## 20-MINUTE SKILLET LASAGNA
### Yield: 4 servings
*Serve with tossed salad with Italian dressing
and Garlicky Toast.*

1 pound ground beef
1 cup frozen chopped onions
1 teaspoon dried basil
1 teaspoon dried oregano
1 teaspoon salt
$\frac{1}{2}$ teaspoon pepper
1 pound frozen cheese ravioli
1½ cups ricotta cheese
1 jar (14 ounces) spaghetti sauce
8 ounces shredded mozzarella cheese

- In a large, heavy skillet, cook and chop the meat and onions until the meat is done, about 10 minutes.
- Drain juices and fat.
- Arrange the frozen pieces of ravioli in the skillet, pushing them down into the cooked meat.
- Dollop the ricotta cheese evenly on top of the ravioli.
- Spread everything with the spaghetti sauce.
- Cover and simmer, without stirring, 10 minutes or until ravioli is done.
- Uncover and sprinkle on the grated cheese.
- Replace the cover, remove from heat, and take to the table.

## LEMON NOODLES
### Yield: 4 servings

1 package (8 ounces) egg noodles (or your favorite pasta)
1 tablespoon olive oil or vegetable oil
1 teaspoon minced garlic
1/4 cup grated Parmesan cheese
Finely grated zest of one lemon
Juice of one lemon
1/2 teaspoon salt
1/4 teaspoon pepper

- Cook noodles according to package directions.
- While the noodles are cooking, heat the oil in a large skillet over medium heat.
- Add garlic and sauté 1 minute.
- Remove skillet from heat. Add cooked, drained noodles and remaining ingredients. Toss well.

MACARONI AND CHEESE FROM THE BOX WILL NEVER HAVE THE CREAMY, CHEESY SOFTNESS OF HOMEMADE. BUT HEY, LIFE ISN'T PERFECT AND SOMETIMES YOU ARE DOING WELL TO GET THE BOXED KIND PUT TOGETHER. IF SO, ADD NUTRIENTS BY THROWING IN SOME CHOPPED LUNCH MEAT LIKE HAM OR TURKEY, A HANDFUL OF FROZEN PEAS, OR TOP THE SERVINGS WITH CHOPPED TOMATOES.

## MACARONI AND CHEESE
### Yield: 4 servings as an entrée

1 package dry macaroni (12 ounces)
2 tablespoons butter
4 ounces processed American cheese, cut into cubes
1 cup grated cheddar cheese
2 tablespoons milk or more if needed
1 teaspoon salt, or to taste
1/2 teaspoon pepper

- Bring a large pot of salted water to a boil. Add macaroni and cook 6 minutes or until just tender.
- Drain macaroni. Return to saucepan and stir in remaining ingredients.
- Stir over low heat until hot and all cheese is melted.

*Baking option: After step 2, pour into buttered baking dish. Sprinkle top with additional cheddar cheese and bake 15 minutes in preheated, 375° oven.*

## MEATBALL HOAGIES
### Yield: 4 servings

*Cooking sliced Italian sausage is a quick way to form meatballs. As the slices cook, their casings shrink and form tasty little semirounds.*

1 pound Italian sausage in casings
2 cups spaghetti sauce
4 sandwich-sized French bread rolls
$\frac{1}{2}$ cup grated Parmesan cheese

- Slice sausage into 1-inch pieces.
- Place sausage pieces in a hot skillet over medium heat. Cook, tossing occasionally, 10 minutes or until sausage is cooked.
- Add spaghetti sauce and bring to a simmer.
- Cut bread lengthwise, but not all the way through.
- Divide the sausage mixture between the four rolls, and top each with Parmesan cheese.
- Serve immediately.

## MEXICAN SKILLET WITH CORN DUMPLINGS
### Yield: 4 large servings

1 pound ground beef
1 envelope taco seasoning mix
$\frac{1}{2}$ cup chopped frozen onion
1 can (1 pound) chopped tomatoes
2 cups frozen corn
1 can (4 ounces) chopped green chilies
1 can (4 ounces) sliced black olives
1 package (10 ounces) corn bread mix

- In a large skillet with a lid, cook and chop ground beef until cooked. Drain any grease.
- Stir in taco mix, onions, tomatoes, corn, chilies, and olives. Cook 2 minutes, stirring often.
- Prepare the corn bread according to package directions, except using half the milk.
- Drop the batter by spoonfuls on top of the meat mixture.
- Cover and simmer 15 minutes or until dumplings are done in the center.

## PASTA PIE
### Yield: 6 servings

*For make-ahead dinner, construct the pie. Cover and store in refrigerator for up to 2 days. Heat at 375° for 20 minutes.*

6 ounces dry pasta (macaroni, spaghetti, or your favorite)
2 eggs, beaten in a small bowl
1 tablespoon olive oil
½ cup Parmesan cheese
4 ounces Polish sausage, thinly sliced
2 cups grated cheddar cheese
2 large tomatoes, thinly sliced
Salt and pepper to taste

- Preheat oven to 375°. Spray a 1-inch pie pan with oil.
- Cook pasta according to package directions.
- When done, drain well and stir in the 2 eggs, olive oil, and Parmesan cheese.
- Place mixture in pie pan and spread with a fork to form a crust.
- Top pasta crust with sliced Polish sausage. Sprinkle on the grated cheese and top with sliced tomatoes. Salt and pepper the tomatoes.
- Place the pie in the preheated oven and bake 20 minutes.
- Serve hot or at room temperature.

*This recipe is great for using up leftovers. Use whatever pasta you have in your pantry. Make it with smoked turkey or other deli meat. Mozzarella cheese or other cheese you happen to have will work as well as cheddar. Make up your own version of Pasta Pie!*

*Low-fat tip:*

*Substitute 3 egg whites for the 2 eggs. Use low-fat sausage and cheese.*

## PASTA PRIMAVERA
### Yield: 4 servings

1 pound linguini
1 tablespoon olive oil
2 medium carrots, peeled and thinly sliced
1 yellow bell pepper, sliced
1 red bell pepper, sliced
2 small zucchini squash, thinly sliced
2 teaspoons minced garlic
1 tablespoon dried marjoram
1 tablespoon dried basil
¼ cup chicken stock
Salt and pepper to taste
½ cup shredded Parmesan cheese

- Cook pasta according to package directions.
- Meanwhile, heat oil in a large skillet over medium-high heat.
- Add vegetables and cook, stirring often until carrots are just tender, about 5 minutes.
- Add marjoram, basil, chicken stock, salt, and pepper. Cook 2 minutes.
- Toss mixture with cooked and drained pasta and Parmesan cheese.

---

*To make buttered bread cubes, spread 4 slices of bread with butter. Stack them together and use a serrated knife to first cut the stack into 4 strips. Turn the stack. Holding the strips together, cut the strips into cubes.*

## HOT CHICKEN SALAD
### Yield: 6 servings

4 cups cooked chicken, diced (about 4 chicken breast halves)
4 cups chopped celery
½ cup chopped green bell pepper
½ cup sliced green onions (about 4 green onions)
½ cup slivered almonds
1 cup shredded cheddar cheese
2 tablespoons chopped pimentos
1 cup mayonnaise
1 cup sour cream
2 cups buttered bread cubes (unbaked croutons)

- Preheat oven to 400°. Lightly spray a 2-quart casserole with vegetable oil.
- Stir together all ingredients except bread cubes.
- Spoon into prepared casserole and top with bread cubes.
- Bake 20 minutes or until hot and bubbly.

### PEPPERONI PIZZA ROLL
Yield: 4 to 6 servings

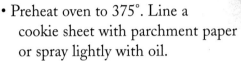

1 loaf frozen bread dough, thawed
½ cup pizza or spaghetti sauce
4 ounces sliced pepperoni
½ cup shredded mozzarella cheese
1 egg, beaten together with
    1 tablespoon water
    to make an egg wash

• Preheat oven to 375°. Line a
    cookie sheet with parchment paper
    or spray lightly with oil.
• On a lightly floured surface, use a rolling pin
    to roll the thawed bread dough into a large rectangle,
    about 12 x 15 inches.
• Spread surface of dough with pizza sauce, leaving a 1-inch border around the edges.
• Arrange the pepperoni and cheese evenly on top of the pizza sauce.
• Starting at one long end, roll the dough, jelly-roll style, pinching the ends together
    to seal in the fillings.
• Place roll on prepared pan and brush top of roll with egg wash.
• Bake 20 minutes or until golden brown.

*Try these optional ingredient ideas or make up your own Pizza Roll:*

    Thinly sliced ham with Swiss cheese and mustard
    Sliced cooked beef with horseradish
    Thinly sliced turkey with blue cheese
    Sliced bell peppers, onions, artichoke hearts, and tomatoes
    Sun-dried tomatoes, fresh basil, and mozzarella cheese
    The ideas are endless!

### Freeze Ahead!

Prepare several of these rolls, up through step 6. Place rolls on a baking
sheet which is lined with wax paper or parchment paper. Place in freezer.
When frozen, wrap each roll in freezer wrap and store in the freezer. To
bake, allow frozen roll to defrost. (It's okay if it's not completely thawed.)
Bake as directed.

## POLISH DINNER
### Yield: 6 servings

*Serve with a good loaf of rye or sourdough bread and fruit salad or tossed salad.*
*Put the mustard in a cute bowl or leftover crock from the cheese spread*
*you got for Christmas last year.*

1 pound sauerkraut
6 to 8 medium new potatoes, cut in half
1 large onion, coarsely chopped
1 pound Polish kielbasa sausage, cut into 2-inch slices
1 cup water
Good mustard (we like brown and grainy) for serving

- Place all ingredients in a soup pot.
- Cover pot and simmer mixture 20 minutes or until potatoes and onions are as tender as you want them.
- Pile on a large, deep platter. Serve with a crock of mustard.

*This is an easy one-dish meal. Sometimes I simmer it so*
*long, some of the potatoes dissolve and help to thicken the mixture.*

## QUICK CORN AND CHEESE CHOWDER
### Yield: 8 servings

3 pieces bacon
2 cans (17 ounces each) cream-style corn
4 cups whole milk
3 cups frozen, diced hash brown potatoes
2 green onions, chopped
Salt and pepper to taste
1 cup grated cheddar cheese

- Fry the bacon until very crisp. Drain well and crumble.
- While the bacon is frying, combine corn, milk, potatoes, onions, salt, and pepper in a large saucepan.
- Heat until just simmering.
- Stir in bacon and cheese and heat until hot and bubbly.

## QUICK AND EASY CRAB SOUP
### Yield: 4 servings

2 tablespoons butter
$\frac{1}{2}$ cup finely chopped onion
1 teaspoon minced garlic
1 tablespoon minced parsley
$\frac{1}{2}$ teaspoon salt
$\frac{1}{4}$ teaspoon pepper
$\frac{1}{2}$ teaspoon dried basil
1 can ($10\frac{3}{4}$ ounces) tomato soup
$1\frac{1}{4}$ cups half-and-half or milk
4 ounces fresh or frozen crabmeat

- Melt butter in a soup pot. Sauté onion and garlic until onion is tender, about 3 minutes.
- Add parsley, salt, basil, soup, and half-and-half. Bring to a simmer. Allow to simmer 5 minutes.
- Stir in crabmeat and allow to heat through.

## 15-MINUTE RICE PILAF
### Yield: 6 servings

2 tablespoons butter
1 cup broken angel-hair pasta*
2 cups instant rice
4 cups water
2 chicken bouillon cubes (enough for 4 cups water)

- Melt butter in a large skillet with a lid, over medium heat.
- Add broken angel-hair pasta, and cook and stir for 3 minutes or until pasta is golden brown.
- Add rice, water, and bouillon cubes. Cover and cook 7 to 10 minutes or until rice and pasta are done.
- Fluff with a fork and serve immediately.

*Break the pasta into pieces about 1-inch long. It doesn't matter if it is in various lengths, just so it is broken enough to stir and cook. If you have a few extra minutes, you can sauté 1 cup chopped onions and bell peppers before adding the broken pasta.*

## BAKED SALMON FILLETS
### Yield: 4 servings
*Serve the salmon with Parsley Potatoes and a tossed salad.*

1¾ to 2 pounds salmon fillets
2 tablespoons olive oil or sesame oil
2 teaspoons salt
1 teaspoon pepper
Juice of one lemon, about 3 tablespoons

- Preheat oven to 475°. Spray a baking sheet with vegetable oil.
- Slice the salmon fillet into ½-inch pieces and lay them in a single layer on the prepared baking sheet.
- Brush the top of each with some olive oil. Sprinkle each piece with salt and pepper.
- Drizzle with lemon juice.
- Bake 5 minutes or until the middle of the thickest piece is flaky and done.

## FISH CAKES
### Yield: 6 servings

*Growing up, we called our tuna cakes Tuna Croquettes.*

1 cup frozen chopped onions and peppers
1 pound canned tuna, salmon, or crab or 1 pound fresh
  crabmeat
½ cup crushed saltine crackers or bread crumbs
¼ cup finely chopped fresh parsley
2 eggs
Juice of one lemon, about 3 tablespoons
1 tablespoon Worcestershire sauce
1 teaspoon salt
½ teaspoon pepper
2 to 4 tablespoons vegetable oil

- Place frozen onions and peppers on a cutting board and
  use a knife to chop fine.
- Place all ingredients in a large bowl and stir until well
  mixed. (It works best to use your hands!)
- Form the mixture into 6 to 8 patties, about ½-inch
  thick.
- Heat the vegetable oil in a large skillet and sauté the
  patties over medium heat until golden brown, about 3 to
  4 minutes on each side.

*This recipe calls for 1 pound of fish, but it's okay if the amount is a little less or a little more, depending on the size of cans you are using. If the mixture seems a little dry or won't hold together to form patties, add a tablespoon or so of mayonnaise to the mixture.*

## Knife Tip

*When cutting round food, like tomatoes, first make a flat edge to work with. Cut the tomato in half and lay each half on its flat surface. Use a serrated knife to make several slices ½ inch apart in one direction, then turn the tomato and make crosswise cuts, again ½ inch apart. Repeat with the second half of tomato.*

## QUICK SUMMER TOMATO SAUCE FOR PASTA

### Yield: about 4½ cups to serve 3 to 4, enough for 4 cups cooked pasta

4 large ripe tomatoes, cut into ½-inch cubes, or
    1 can (28 ounces) chopped tomatoes
1 small package fresh basil, chopped (about 1 cup)
1 teaspoon dried oregano
2 teaspoons minced garlic
¼ cup extra-virgin olive oil
1 small onion, grated
1 teaspoon salt
½ teaspoon pepper
½ cup grated Parmesan cheese

- Combine all ingredients in a large bowl.
- If time permits, allow to sit for awhile to combine flavors.

*Start a pot (with a lid) of water heating over high heat before you start this sauce. As soon as it comes to a boil, add dry pasta. By the time you get the sauce ready, the pasta will be cooked. (Most pasta takes about 6 minutes to cook* al dente.*)*

## TACO PIE

Yield: 6 servings

*For Chicken Taco Pie, stir 1 pound cooked and chopped chicken into taco sauce.*

1 pound ground beef, browned and drained
2 tablespoons packaged dry taco seasoning mix
   (or to taste)
1 bag (12 ounces) corn chips
Chopped lettuce, onion, and tomatoes
1 cup grated cheddar cheese
Taco sauce for serving

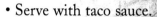

- Stir together the browned meat and dry taco seasoning.
- Spoon cooked and seasoned meat over corn chips. Top with lettuce, onion, tomatoes, and cheese.
- Serve with taco sauce.

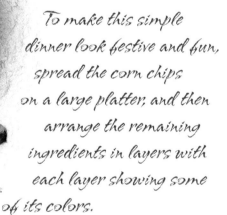

*To make this simple dinner look festive and fun, spread the corn chips on a large platter, and then arrange the remaining ingredients in layers with each layer showing some of its colors.*

*Large platters make food look more important and delicious!*

## COUNTRY VEGETABLE PIES
### Yield: 2 pies to serve 6 to 8

2 prepared piecrusts
4 ounces cream cheese, softened
1 cup grated Swiss cheese
4 cups frozen stir-fry vegetable mixture
2 tablespoons vegetable oil
1 tablespoon dried basil
1 teaspoon salt
$\frac{1}{2}$ teaspoon pepper
1 egg, beaten with 1 tablespoon
    water to make an egg wash

- Preheat oven to 375°. Line two
   baking sheets with parchment
   paper or spray with nonstick coating.
- Place 1 piecrust on each baking sheet.
- Beat together the cream cheese and
   Swiss cheese. Spread half on each
   piecrust, leaving a 2-inch border of dough.
- Toss the vegetables with the vegetable oil,
   basil, salt, and pepper.
- Place half the vegetables on each crust, covering the cheese mixture.
- Fold up the edges of the dough, partially covering the filling.
   Press the edges together to hold them in place.
- Use a pastry brush to cover dough with egg wash.
- Bake 20 minutes or until golden. Serve warm.

*This recipe makes 2 open-faced pies that are great
left over and reheated. Substitute or add any vegetables
you have on hand! This is a great way to get kids to eat vegetables.*

CHAPTER SIX
*Snacks and Desserts*

# Snacks and Desserts

*Is* there anything more homey than the smell of cookies baking in the oven? Or a big, three-layer cake frosted in creamy chocolate icing? Delicious desserts seem to add the exclamation points to dinners and parties. A plate of No-Bake Cookies is quick to make and will say to your family, "You deserve a homemade treat!"

Desserts add a great look and feel to your kitchen! It's easy to make cookies look snazzy—just arrange them on a platter. And cakes can look spectacular just by serving them on a footed cake plate.

I was grown before I realized why my mom baked cookies at 3:00 in the afternoon. "I wanted you to smell cookies baking when you came in from school," she finally told me one day. Well, in these days, it's not always possible for Mom to be baking at that time of day. But you can still create the same effect for your kids. Keep a batch of Oatmeal Cookie Mix, or a roll of refrigerated cookie dough from the grocery store, in the refrigerator and bake up a few while they are doing homework. The warm aroma of baking cookies will bring them running to the kitchen. And you will have created a great memory—that Mom baked cookies for them while they were doing schoolwork!

Here are all my favorite recipes, and I hope they add sweetness and happiness to your home!

# Survival Pantry

## DRY PANTRY:

Brown sugar
White sugar
Powdered sugar
Flour
Self-rising flour
Biscuit mix
Cake mixes—white and chocolate
Vegetable shortening
Peanut butter
Chocolate chips
Unsweetened chocolate
Cocoa powder
Pecans or other nuts
Coconut
Oatmeal
Crispy flake dry cereal
Marshmallows
Graham crackers
Chocolate cookies and vanilla wafers
    for crumbs
Canned fruit
Pie filling
Canned apple slices
Cranberry sauce
Light corn syrup
Sweetened condensed milk
Evaporated milk
Gelatin in various flavors
Vanilla
Almond flavoring
Baking soda
Baking powder

## FROZEN PANTRY:

Orange juice
Raspberries and strawberries
Prepared piecrusts
Baked angel food cake
Peppermint ice cream
Whipped topping

## REFRIGERATOR PANTRY:

Butter
Eggs
Cream cheese
Yogurt
Sour cream
Maraschino cherries

## Parchment Paper

*Lining cookie sheets with parchment keeps them clean and new looking. It may also be used under pies to catch drips.*

## NO-BAKE CHOCOLATE COOKIES
### Yield: 2 dozen cookies

2 cups sugar
⅓ cup cocoa
½ cup butter (1 stick)
½ cup milk
½ cup creamy peanut butter
3 cups instant oatmeal, uncooked
1 teaspoon vanilla

- Line cookie sheets with wax paper or parchment paper.
- In a saucepan mix the sugar, cocoa, butter, and milk. Place over medium heat.
- Bring to a boil, stirring constantly. Allow to boil 2 whole minutes.
- Remove from heat and stir in peanut butter, oatmeal, and vanilla.
- Drop by spoonfuls onto lined cookie sheets.
- Let cool to set.

*This cookbook for busy moms would not be complete without these incredibly easy cookies! My mother-in-law made the recipe a family heirloom, as it's been passed down for four generations now. Half candy, half cookie, they are addictive! They pack well and are great for trips or campouts—so are the Crunchies that follow.*

## NO-BAKE PEANUT BUTTER CRUNCHIES
### Yield: 2 dozen crunchies

1 cup light corn syrup
1 cup sugar
2 cups creamy peanut butter
4 cups Special K cereal or other
   crispy flake cereal

- Line cookie sheets with wax paper or
  parchment paper.
- In a saucepan, bring sugar and syrup to a boil.
- Remove from heat and stir in peanut butter
  until smooth.
- Stir in cereal.
- Drop by spoonfuls onto lined cookie sheets.
  Let cool to set.

*Measuring powdered sugar, flour, and cocoa:*

To accurately measure these ingredients, use a "dry" measuring cup.
This is a measuring cup that when full to the rim holds the exact amount appropriate.
It is usually metal or plastic. Lightly spoon the ingredient into the measuring cup
and level it off with a straight edge, such as the back of a knife or metal spatula.
Tapping the cup and adding more dry ingredients
will make an inaccurate measurement.

WHEN BAKED COOKIES ARE REMOVED FROM THE OVEN, LET THEM SIT ON THE BAKING SHEET ABOUT 45 SECONDS BEFORE REMOVING TO A RACK OR COUNTER TO COOL. IF YOU LET THEM SIT ANY LONGER, THEY MIGHT COOL AND STICK TO THE BAKING SHEET. IF THIS HAPPENS, IT IS EASY TO CORRECT. SIMPLY PUT THEM BACK IN THE OVEN FOR 45 SECONDS TO SOFTEN UP, AND THEY WILL LIFT OFF THE BAKING SHEET EASILY.

## CHOCOLATE CHUNK COOKIE MONSTERS
### Yield: 1 dozen
*These are huge cookies that are fun to eat.*
*Serve with cold milk!*

½ cup butter
⅓ cup peanut butter
½ cup white sugar
½ cup brown sugar
1 egg
1 teaspoon vanilla
1 cup plus 2 tablespoons flour
½ teaspoon baking soda
2 cups chocolate chunks
1 cup chopped pecans, optional

- Preheat oven to 325°. Lightly spray baking sheets with vegetable oil or line with parchment paper.
- In a mixer bowl, beat together the butter, peanut butter, and sugars until light and fluffy.
- Beat in the eggs and vanilla.
- Stir together the flour and baking soda. Add to the creamed mixture and beat until thoroughly mixed.
- Form ¼-cup mounds of dough on prepared baking sheets.
- Push chocolate chunks and pecans into mounds.
- Bake 15 minutes or until just lightly browned.
- Remove from oven and allow cookies to rest on baking sheet for 1 minute before removing with a large metal spatula.

## WHITE CHOCOLATE CHIP AND MACADAMIA COOKIES
### Yield: 4 dozen

¾ cup butter
1 cup brown sugar
2 eggs
1 teaspoon vanilla
2½ cups flour
1 teaspoon baking soda
1 teaspoon salt
2 cups white chocolate chips
1 cup chopped macadamia nuts

• Preheat oven to 350°.
• Spray cookie sheets with vegetable oil or line with parchment paper.
• In a large mixing bowl, beat butter and sugar until light and fluffy.
• Add eggs and vanilla. Beat for 1 minute.
• Stir together flour, baking soda, and salt. Add to the butter mixture. Beat well.
• Stir in white chocolate chips and macadamia nuts.
• Use a teaspoon to drop dollops of dough onto prepared baking sheets.
• Bake 12 to 15 minutes, or until lightly browned.

## INSTANT OATMEAL COOKIES

2 cups Instant Oatmeal Cookie Mix (recipe below)
1 egg
1 teaspoon vanilla
1 cup raisins

- Preheat oven to 350°. Line cookie sheets with parchment paper or spray with vegetable oil.
- Place Cookie Mix in a mixer bowl. Add egg and vanilla. Mix until well blended.
- Stir in raisins.
- Drop by spoonfuls onto prepared cookie sheets.
- Bake 8 to 10 minutes or until just beginning to brown.

### INSTANT OATMEAL COOKIE MIX
Yield: 4 quarts of mix

3 cups flour
2 teaspoons salt
2 teaspoons baking soda
1 teaspoon baking powder
2 cups sugar
2 cups brown sugar
2 cups butter or vegetable shortening
6 cups instant oatmeal

- Combine flour, salt, baking soda, baking powder, sugar, and brown sugar. Stir to combine well.
- Add butter. Blend by hand or mixer until crumbly.
- Stir in oatmeal.
- Store in plastic bags, jars, or plastic containers in the refrigerator for up to 3 months or freezer for 6 months.

## BUTTERY SUGAR COOKIES
### Yield: 4 dozen cookies

*If you are a sugar-cookie fanatic like I am, you will love these!*
*They taste like old-fashioned homemade vanilla ice cream.*

1 cup butter
2 cups sugar
2 eggs
2 tablespoons milk
1 teaspoon vanilla
3 cups flour
2 teaspoons baking powder
$\frac{1}{2}$ teaspoon salt

- In a mixing bowl, beat together the butter and sugar until light and fluffy.
- Add eggs and milk. Beat until smooth.
- Stir together the flour, baking powder, and salt. Beat into mixture.
- Divide mixture into four parts, placing each part on plastic wrap and wrapping tightly. Refrigerate at least 1 hour or until firm.
- Preheat oven to 350°. Lightly spray baking sheets with vegetable oil or line with parchment paper.
- On a floured surface, roll out chilled dough to $\frac{1}{4}$-inch thick. Cut out cookies with 2-inch round cookie cutter
- Place cookies on prepared pans and bake 6 to 8 minutes or until just beginning to brown.

*The dough is so tender it will not keep the shape of a cookie cutter.*
*For shaped cookies, use Judie's Favorite Sugar Cookies.*

## GELATIN COOKIE PRESS COOKIES
Yield: 5 dozen pressed cookies

1½ cups butter
1 package (3 ounces) gelatin, dry
1 cup sugar
1 egg
1 teaspoon vanilla
4 cups flour
1 teaspoon baking powder
Pinch of salt

> *Making cookies with a cookie press is a fun way to spend time with your children. Let them choose the color and flavor of gelatin for this recipe.*

- Preheat oven to 350°.
- In a mixing bowl, beat the butter, sugar, and gelatin until light and fluffy.
- Add egg and vanilla and beat until smooth.
- Stir together the flour, baking powder, and salt. Beat this into the butter mixture.
- Form with cookie press onto ungreased cookie sheets.
- Bake 8 to 10 minutes or until just beginning to brown.

## SPRITZ

Yield: 4 dozen cookies

*You can divide Spritz dough and use cake coloring to make various colors of cookies.*

1 cup butter
½ cup sugar
1 teaspoon vanilla
1 teaspoon almond flavoring
1 egg
2¼ cups flour
½ teaspoon salt

- Preheat oven to 350°.
- Beat together butter, sugar, vanilla, almond flavoring, and egg.
- Stir together dry ingredients and add to butter mixture. Mix well.
- Fill cookie press with ¼ of the dough at a time, and form shapes on ungreased baking sheets.
- Bake 5 to 7 minutes or until set but not browned.

## FROSTED CHOCOLATE COOKIES
Yield: 2 dozen

½ cup vegetable oil
1 cup light brown sugar
1 egg
2 ounces unsweetened chocolate, melted
1 teaspoon vanilla
1¾ cup flour
2 teaspoons baking powder
½ teaspoon salt
½ cup milk
Chopped pecans

- Preheat oven to 350°. Spray cookie sheets with vegetable oil or line with parchment.
- In a mixing bowl, beat together the oil, brown sugar, and egg.
- Beat in melted chocolate and vanilla.
- Stir together the flour, baking powder, and salt. Add to creamed mixture, along with milk.
- Stir in pecans.
- Drop by large teaspoonfuls onto prepared pans.
- Bake 10 minutes.
- Remove from oven and cool before frosting.

## CHOCOLATE COOKIE FROSTING

3 tablespoons butter
2 ounces unsweetened chocolate
1½ cups unsifted powdered sugar
¼ cup boiling water
½ teaspoon vanilla
⅛ teaspoon salt

- Place butter and chocolate in a saucepan and melt over low heat, stirring constantly.
- Add remaining ingredients and stir until very smooth.
- Add more water, if needed, for spreading consistency.

IF YOU ARE BAKING WITH 2 PANS IN THE OVEN AT ONCE, SWITCH THE PANS ON THE RACKS AFTER THE FIRST 4 MINUTES OF BAKING. THIS WILL ASSURE THE TOPS AND BOTTOMS OF THE COOKIES WILL BE BAKED EVENLY.

## MOM'S FAMOUS CHOCOLATE CHIP COOKIES
Yield: 8 dozen cookies

*This is my family's favorite cookie recipe.*
*They say it has made me famous with them!*

1 cup butter
1 cup vegetable shortening
1½ cups white sugar
1½ cups brown sugar
1 tablespoon vanilla
4 eggs
4½ cups flour
2 teaspoons baking soda
2 teaspoons salt
2 packages (12 ounces each) chocolate chips

- Preheat oven to 350°. Spray baking sheets with vegetable oil or line with parchment.
- Beat together the butter, shortening, sugars, and vanilla until light and fluffy.
- Beat in eggs. Stir together the flour, baking soda, and salt. Add to the creamed mixture and beat well.
- Stir in chocolate chips.
- Drop by spoonfuls (about 1-inch wide) onto prepared baking sheets.
- Bake 8 to 10 minutes or until lightly browned.

*These freeze very well for up to 2 months in airtight containers.*

## JUDIE'S FAVORITE SUGAR COOKIES
### Yield: 3 dozen 2-inch cookies

1 cup butter
2 cups sugar
2 eggs
2 tablespoons maple syrup
1 teaspoon vanilla
4 cups flour
½ teaspoon salt
1 teaspoon baking powder

- In an electric mixer, beat together
  the butter and sugar until
  light and fluffy.
- Add eggs, maple syrup, and vanilla.
  Beat well. Scrape down sides of bowl.
- Stir together all dry ingredients. Add a little
  at a time to the butter mixture, mixing until well blended.
- Divide dough into 3 parts and wrap each in plastic wrap,
  forming dough into a large, flat disk. Refrigerate at least 1 hour.
- Preheat oven to 350°. Line cookie sheets with parchment
  paper or spray with vegetable oil.
- On a lightly floured board, roll out one of the disks to about ⅛-inch thickness and
  cut out with cookie cutters.
- Put shapes on prepared sheets and bake for 8 minutes or until just beginning to
  brown around the edges.
- Remove from oven and cool on racks or your countertop.

*These cookies freeze well, even when frosted. A great icing recipe
for these cookies is on page 220.
Make sure they are in airtight freezer containers
or freezer zipper bags. Freeze for up to 2 months.*

## ROYAL ICING

*This is the icing that turns hard when it dries.*
*Cookies frosted with it may be stacked or even packed and mailed.*

3 tablespoons meringue powder (available at craft stores with cake decorating supplies)
4 cups sifted powdered sugar (about 1 pound)
5 to 6 tablespoons water
Paste food coloring (available with the meringue powder)

• Beat together all ingredients until light and fluffy, about 7 minutes.
• Add food coloring as desired.

*This icing may be thinned with a few drops of water and used to "paint"*
*the entire tops of the cookies.*

## CHOCOLATE FUDGE COOKIES

Yield: about 3 dozen cookies

7 ounces semisweet chocolate
2 ounces unsweetened chocolate
3 tablespoons butter
1 cup sugar
3 eggs
2 teaspoons strong coffee
3/4 teaspoon vanilla
3/4 cup flour
1/2 teaspoon baking powder
1/4 teaspoon salt
4 ounces semisweet chocolate, coarsely chopped
3/4 cup chopped pecans

• Preheat oven to 350°. Line cookie sheets with parchment paper or spray with
  vegetable oil.
• In a heavy saucepan over low heat, melt first two chocolates and butter. Set aside.
• In a mixing bowl, cream sugar and eggs.
• Mix in coffee and vanilla.
• Stir together flour, baking powder, and salt. Stir into chocolate mixture.
• Stir in chopped chocolate and pecans.
• Drop onto cookie sheets and bake 12 minutes or until tops are shiny and cracked.

## PERFECT FUDGE BROWNIES
### Yield: 16 brownies
*When making brownies, grease only the bottom of the pan so the batter*
*can cling to the sides and rise.*

½ cup butter
1 cup sugar
2 eggs
2 ounces unsweetened chocolate, melted
1 teaspoon vanilla
½ cup flour
½ cup chopped pecans or walnuts

• Preheat oven to 325°. Grease bottom only of an 8 x 8-inch baking dish.
• In a large bowl, cream butter and sugar.
• Add eggs and beat well.
• Blend in melted chocolate, vanilla, and flour.
• Stir in nuts.
• Pour batter into prepared pan and bake 35 minutes.
• Frost with Cooked Fudge Frosting.

## COOKED FUDGE FROSTING

2 ounces unsweetened chocolate
3 cups sugar
3 tablespoons corn syrup
¼ teaspoon salt
1 cup milk
¼ cup butter (½ stick)
1 teaspoon vanilla

• In a medium saucepan, heat the chocolate, sugar, corn syrup, salt, and milk.
• Cook over low heat, stirring until sugar dissolves.
• Continue cooking to soft-ball stage (232° on a candy thermometer).
• Remove from heat; add butter and vanilla.
• Beat until frosting cools and is of spreading consistency.

## Melting Chocolate

Chocolate will seize up if melted at too high a temperature. To prevent this, heat in a double boiler, where the heat is very gentle. If you don't have a double boiler, put a small saucepan inside a larger one. Fill the bottom with water so it almost touches the top pan, but not quite. Place the chocolate in the top pan. Heat the water to a simmer, and stir the chocolate as it melts.

*Microwave method:* Melt chopped chocolate at medium for 1 minute. Stir chocolate, even though it may still be mostly solid. Melt for 30 seconds at a time, stirring after each melting. When chocolate is shiny and melting, remove from microwave and stir until completely melted.

### BROWNIE BOOSTERS
*Add even more goodness to any packaged brownie mix or recipe
by adding one or more of the following:*

$3/4$ cup cubed chocolate candy bars, such as Milky Ways, Almond Joys, or Peter Paul Mounds

$3/4$ cup chocolate-covered raisins or peanuts

$1/2$ cup dried cherries

$1/2$ cup diced glazed or chocolate-covered orange peel

$2/3$ cup miniature marshmallows

$1/2$ cup macadamia or other nuts, in addition to nuts already called for in the recipe

## COCONUT COOKIE BARS
### Yield: 15 to 20 bars
*This recipe is simple to make—and oh! so rich to eat!*

*1st layer:*
2 cups flour
½ teaspoon salt
1 cup brown sugar
⅔ cup butter
2 eggs

- Preheat oven to 425°. Spray a 9 x 13-inch baking pan with vegetable oil.
- In a large bowl, stir together flour, salt, and sugar.
- Add butter and mix well.
- Add eggs and mix again.
- Spread into bottom of prepared baking pan.
- Bake 6 to 8 minutes or until lightly browned.

*2nd layer:*
2 cups brown sugar
¼ cup flour
½ teaspoon salt
½ teaspoon baking powder
2 eggs
2 teaspoons vanilla
1 cup coconut

- Reduce oven to 350°.
- Stir together brown sugar, flour, salt, and baking powder.
- Stir in vanilla and coconut.
- Spread evenly on baked crust and return to oven for 25 minutes or until lightly browned.
- Remove from oven. When cool, cut into bars.

## CHOCOLATE PEANUT BUTTER TREATS
Yield: 16 small squares
*Cut them small—you only need a little!*

1 cup peanut butter
½ cup sugar
1 egg
1 package (4 ounces) German chocolate, broken into pieces

- Preheat oven to 325°.
- Beat peanut butter, sugar, and egg until well blended.
- Spread into an 8 x 8-inch baking pan. Bake 15 minutes.
- Remove from the oven. Sprinkle on the chocolate pieces.
- Cover hot pan with foil and allow to stand 3 minutes.
- Remove foil and spread melted chocolate evenly over surface.
- Immediately cut into squares.

---

## CARAMEL CREAM CHEESE BARS
Yield: 24 bars

½ cup butter, melted
1 package yellow or butter-flavored cake mix, dry
1 cup firmly packed brown sugar
2 packages (8 ounces each) cream cheese

- Preheat oven to 350°.
- For the crust, in a medium bowl, stir together the butter and cake mix until well mixed.
- Spread in bottom of 9 x 13-inch baking dish.
- Use a mixer to cream brown sugar and cream cheese.
- Spread mixture over crust.
- Bake 20 minutes or until golden brown.

*These caramel bars are from my sister-in-law, who makes them to take to work. Everyone who eats them can't believe they are so easy to make.*

## QUICK CREAMY FUDGE
Yield: 24 pieces of candy

*For fancy fudge, make score marks with a knife
where you are going to cut the fudge.
Lightly press a pecan half on each one.*

3 packages (12 ounces each) chocolate chips
1 cup butter
2 cups chopped pecans, optional
8 ounces miniature marshmallows
4½ cups sugar
1 can (12 ounces) evaporated milk

• Generously butter two 9 x 13-inch glass baking pans.
• In a large, heat-proof bowl, place the chocolate chips, butter, pecans, and marshmallows. Set aside.
• Place sugar and evaporated milk in a saucepan. Simmer 10 minutes.
• Pour hot mixture over ingredients in bowl and stir until smooth.
• Pour into prepared pans and allow to cool.
• Refrigerate several hours or until firm. Slice into serving pieces.

## CHOCOLATE BIRDS' NESTS
Yield: 2 dozen

1 package (12 ounces) chocolate chips
1 package (12 ounces) butterscotch chips
1 can (6 ounces) chow mein noodles
Jellybeans

• Melt chocolate chips and butterscotch chips together in a medium-sized saucepan.
• Stir chow mein noodles into melted chocolate mixture.
• Drop by spoonfuls onto wax paper, and spread with a spoon to look like nests.
• Press three jellybeans into the tops of each to resemble eggs in the nests.
• Allow to cool and become firm.

## Dad's Tradition

*My daughter-in-law's dad raised two daughters. Each Christmas season, the three of them make fudge together in the kitchen. Mom takes the pictures! Now this tradition is being passed on as our granddaughter gets in on the action.*

*Maybe you can start a similar tradition in your home. It's never too late to start!*

## CHOCOLATE-FROSTED CREAM PUFFS
### Yield: 12 cream puffs

*You can use pudding in the cream puffs instead of whipped cream.*

1 recipe Cream Puff Batter
1 recipe Sweetened Whipped Cream
  (recipe on next page)
1 can prepared chocolate frosting or your
  favorite frosting recipe

- Preheat oven to 400°.
- Use a serving spoon to plop 12 mounds of
  dough onto an ungreased cookie sheet.
- Bake 20 minutes or until outside is dry
  and golden brown.
- Allow puffs to cool completely.
- Use a serrated knife to cut off the top
  ¼ of each puff.
- Pull out the wet dough pieces from
  inside each puff.
- Fill each puff with whipped cream.
- Frost each lid with 1 tablespoon of the
  frosting and place on top of filled bottoms.
- Refrigerate until ready to serve.

## CREAM PUFF BATTER

1 cup water
½ cup butter
1 cup flour
4 eggs

- Preheat oven to 400°.
- In a medium-size saucepan,
  heat the water and butter
  until it comes to a rolling boil.
- Add the flour to the boiling
  water and stir vigorously over
  low heat until the mixture
  forms a ball, about 1 minute.
- Remove the pan from the heat
  and beat in all the eggs at one
  time. The mixture will be
  lumpy at first, but keep beating until the batter becomes
  smooth and satiny.
- Use a large spoon to drop
  mounds (about ¼ cup) of the
  batter onto ungreased baking
  sheets.
- Bake 32 to 35 minutes or until
  puffs are golden brown and
  dry, then remove from oven
  and let cool.
- Cut off the tops and pull out
  filaments of soft dough.
- Fill cream puffs with whipped
  cream, pudding, chicken salad,
  or filling of your choice.

## FRESH FRUIT WITH CREAM CHEESE DIP
### Yield: 4 servings

3 ounces cream cheese, softened
1 tablespoon milk
1 tablespoon sugar-free strawberry jam
4 cups fruit, such as strawberries, apple or peach slices

- Combine cream cheese, milk, and jam. Beat until smooth.
- Place dip in a bowl on a platter. Surround with fruit for dipping.

## SWEETENED WHIPPED CREAM
### Yield: 4 cups

2 cups heavy cream
2 tablespoons sugar, or to taste
1 teaspoon vanilla

• Place all ingredients in a mixing bowl and beat with an electric mixer until peaks form.
• Taste whipped cream. Stir in more sugar if needed.

### Everyone Loves Whipped Cream!

*You can whip the cream from scratch, buy the can, use prepared whipped topping, or mix two together! Serve a dollop on top of pancakes, waffles, ice cream, or yogurt. Use it to fill cream puffs or frost a cake. The ideas are many, and you will probably think up some of your own.*

### Whipped Wonder!

*Of course, whipping your own cream from scratch is the very best. Be sure to not overbeat the cream, or it will turn into butter. Beat just until firm peaks form. If you accidentally make butter, save it for breakfast and present it as a special treat for pancakes or toast—homemade butter!*

## FROZEN YOGURT POPS
### Yield: 6 pops

2 cups plain yogurt
1 can (6 ounces) frozen orange juice, undiluted
1 teaspoon vanilla
6 paper cups (4 ounces)
6 Popsicle sticks

• Mix together yogurt, orange juice, and vanilla.
• Pour mixture into paper cups.
• Set a Popsicle stick in the center of each.
• Place on a tray and carefully place in freezer to freeze.
• Peel away the paper cup to eat the yogurt pop.

## SHORTCAKE FRUIT COBBLER
### Yield: 6 servings

2 tablespoons packaged biscuit mix
$\frac{1}{2}$ cup sugar (if you are using unsweetened fruit)
$\frac{1}{2}$ teaspoon cinnamon
$2\frac{1}{2}$ to 3 cups canned fruit with juice
1 tablespoon lemon juice

- Preheat oven to 425°.
- Stir together the biscuit mix, sugar, and cinnamon.
- Stir in the fruit and lemon juice.
- Pour into bottom of 8-inch square baking dish.
- Top with 6 shortcakes.
- Bake 25 minutes or until hot and bubbly
  and shortcakes are light brown.

*Shortcakes:*
1 cup packaged biscuit mix
3 tablespoons boiling water
$\frac{1}{4}$ cup softened butter

- Place biscuit mix in mixing bowl and pour
  on the boiling water.
- Add softened butter and stir vigorously with a fork until the dough holds together.
  The dough will be puffy and soft.
- Divide into 6 parts and lightly press each into a round biscuit shape.

## QUICK AND EASY FRUIT COBBLER
### Yield: one 9 x 13-inch cobbler to serve 8 to 10

1⅓ cups self-rising flour
1⅓ cups sugar
1 cup milk
1 stick butter, melted
2 cans (15 ounces each) pie filling, such as apple or cherry

• Preheat oven to 350°. Spray a 9 x 13-inch baking dish with vegetable oil.
• Beat together the flour, sugar, and milk.
• Pour into bottom of prepared baking dish.
• Pour melted butter on top.
• Spoon pie filling over all.
• Bake 55 minutes.

---

## QUICK FRUIT CRISP

1 can pie filling

*Topping:*
½ cup brown sugar
½ cup oatmeal
½ cup flour
¾ teaspoon cinnamon
¾ teaspoon nutmeg
⅓ cup butter

• Preheat oven to 375°. Lightly spray an 8-inch cake pan with vegetable oil.
• Spread pie filling into the bottom of the prepared cake pan.
• In a medium bowl, stir together brown sugar, oatmeal, flour, cinnamon, and nutmeg.
• Use a knife or pastry cutter to cut the butter into the dry mixture until it is crumbly.
• Spread crumbly mixture evenly over the pie filling.
• Bake 20 minutes or until hot, bubbly, and golden brown.

IF YOU ARE IN A REAL PINCH FOR TIME, YOU CAN USE A CAN OF PIE FILLING—ANY FLAVOR. STIR IN ½ TEASPOON CINNAMON AND ½ TEASPOON ALMOND FLAVORING OR 1 TEASPOON ORANGE ZEST TO MAKE IT TASTE MORE HOMEMADE!

## QUICK APPLE RASPBERRY TART
### Yield: 4 to 6 servings
*For this pie, you don't even take time to use a pie pan!*
*Just form the two-layer pie on a baking sheet.*

1 package ready-made piecrusts
¼ cup flour
1 cup sugar
1 can apple slices (not apple pie filling)
1 cup frozen raspberries
3 tablespoons butter
1 egg, beaten with 1 tablespoon water to make an egg wash

- Preheat oven to 375°.
- Lay one piecrust on a baking sheet.
- In a large bowl, stir together the flour and sugar.
- Add apple slices and raspberries. Toss to coat well.
- Pile fruit and flour mixture in the center of the piecrust, leaving a 1-inch border around the edges.
- Dot butter over fruit.
- Lay second piecrust on top, and pinch edges all around to hold in all the juices as the tart bakes.
- Brush top with egg wash.
- Bake for 35 minutes or until crust is golden brown.

## CHOCOLATE PECAN PIE
### Yield: one 8-inch pie
*This recipe if tripled will fill two 9-inch, deep-dish pie shells.*

8-inch piecrust
½ cup butter
½ cup chocolate chips
1 cup sugar
2 eggs, beaten together in a small bowl
½ cup chopped pecans
½ cup coconut

- Preheat oven to 350°.
- Line an 8-inch pie pan with the piecrust. Refrigerate piecrust until ready to fill.
- In a saucepan or microwave-proof bowl, melt the butter.
- Add chocolate chips. Stir until melted and smooth.
- Remove from heat. Stir in remaining ingredients.
- Pour into prepared shell.
- Bake 35 minutes.

*My daughter-in-law Stephanie gave me this recipe. Every Christmas, she makes these pies for gifts. She sets the finished pie on a large square of cellophane, ties it up with a ribbon on top, and she and my son deliver them to the lucky and eager friends and neighbors. What a gift!*

*Make Ahead*

*You can make this pie ahead and freeze it. Then plan 1 day for wrapping and delivering. Stephanie says to take the pie out of the oven after 35 minutes, when the center is still a little wet. This way the pie is gooey and good!*

## FROZEN PEPPERMINT PIE
Yield: one 9-inch pie

1½ cups chocolate cookie crumbs
¼ cup butter, melted
1 pint peppermint ice cream
1 container (8 ounces) frozen whipped topping, thawed
¼ cup finely crushed peppermint candy
Peppermint candies for decorating

- Stir together the cookie crumbs and melted butter.
- Press firmly into a 9-inch pie pan.
- Combine peppermint ice cream and whipped topping.
- Spoon ice cream mixture into crust.
- Sprinkle top with crushed peppermint candy.
- Decorate top with additional peppermint candies.
- Freeze pie.

---

## CREAM CHEESE PIE
Yield: one 9-inch pie
*I love this recipe for cream cheese pie. It is so simple, yet very rich and dense.
Top with cherry or apricot pie filling if desired.*

2 packages (8 ounces) cream cheese, softened
¾ cup sugar
2 teaspoons lemon juice
½ teaspoon vanilla
3 eggs
9-inch graham cracker crust

- Preheat oven to 325°.
- Beat together all ingredients until smooth.
- Pour into prepared crust.
- Bake 30 minutes.

## CRANAPPLE PIE
Yield: 1 pie (8- or 9-inch)
*This pie can be frozen after assembling.*
*Allow to defrost before baking according to directions.*

1 package prepared piecrusts
(contains 2 crusts)
1 can (20 ounces) apple slices, drained
(not pie filling)
1 can (16 ounces) whole berry
cranberry sauce
¾ cup sugar
¼ cup flour
2 tablespoons butter
Egg wash: 1 egg beaten together
with 1 tablespoon water

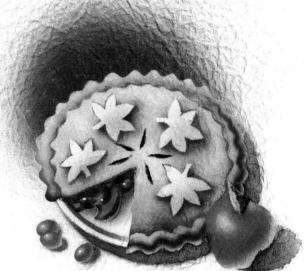

- Preheat oven to 375°.
- Line an 8-inch or 9-inch pie pan with one of the crusts.
- In a large bowl, toss together the apple slices and cranberry sauce.
- In a small bowl, stir together the sugar and flour. Stir this into the apple mixture.
- Pile apple mixture onto piecrust.
- Dot apples with butter.
- Use a rolling pin or sturdy drinking glass to roll out the remaining piecrust, making it a little larger.
- Place this crust on top of the apples, and trim the edges to fit the bottom crust. Keep the trimmed pieces and set aside.
- Use your fingers to crimp the two crusts together around the edges. Use a knife to cut several steam vents in the top crust.
- Reroll the trimmed piecrust pieces and use a leaf-shaped cookie cutter to cut out pastry leaves. Place them on top of the piecrust.
- Brush the top crust and leaves with the egg wash.
- Bake 30 to 35 minutes or until hot and bubbly and golden brown.

*If you don't have a leaf-shaped cookie cutter, use a small knife*
*to cut out smooth-shaped leaves from the pastry.*

TO MAKE CHOCOLATE SLIVERS, SCRAPE A CARROT PEELER ALONG THE SIDE OF A SOLID CHOCOLATE CANDY BAR. PLACE SLIVERS DIRECTLY ON WAX PAPER SO THEY DON'T STICK TO ANY SURFACE. IF THE CHOCOLATE DOESN'T MAKE GREAT SLIVERS, USE WHATEVER SHAPE COMES OUT, AND PRETEND YOU WANTED IT THAT WAY.

## CHOCOLATE TRUFFLE PIE
### Yield: one 9-inch pie

1 cup butter
2 cups powdered sugar
4 squares (1 ounce each) bitter chocolate, melted
4 eggs, beaten with a fork
1 teaspoon peppermint flavoring
2 teaspoons vanilla
Chocolate slivers (see sidebar)
12 green maraschino cherry halves
1 Cookie Piecrust (recipe below) or prepared cookie crust

- In a mixer bowl, beat the butter and powdered sugar until light and fluffy.
- Add the melted chocolate, beaten eggs, peppermint flavoring, and vanilla. Beat 1 minute.
- Pile into Cookie Piecrust.
- Top with whipped cream, chocolate slivers, and green maraschino cherries.

## COOKIE PIECRUST

2 cups crushed vanilla wafers
¼ cup melted butter

- Preheat oven to 350°.
- Stir together the crushed vanilla wafers and melted butter. Spread evenly in a 9-inch pie pan.
- Bake 8 to 10 minutes or until crust begins to brown.
- Remove from oven and cool before adding filling.

## BREAD PUDDING
### Yield: 6 servings

8 cups stale French bread, broken into small pieces
2 cups milk
1½ cups sugar
1 teaspoon cinnamon
5 tablespoons butter, melted
3 eggs
1 tablespoon vanilla
½ cup raisins
½ cup chopped pecans
½ cup shredded coconut

• Preheat oven to 350°. Spray a 2-quart baking dish with vegetable oil.
• Place bread in a large bowl and pour the milk over it.
• Stir several minutes until all bread is soaked.
• Add remaining ingredients and mix well.
• Pour into prepared baking dish and bake 1 hour or until middle is set and top is golden brown.
• Serve with Butter Sauce.

### BUTTER SAUCE

¼ cup butter
¾ cup powdered sugar, sifted
1 egg yolk
¼ cup cream

• Melt the butter in a saucepan over medium heat.
• Add the sugar, and whisk until all the butter is absorbed. Remove from heat.
• Beat the egg yolk into the cream.
• Whisk the egg yolk mixture into the butter mixture, beating until smooth.
• Heat and stir over low heat until hot.
• Pour over individual servings of warm bread pudding.

## BUTTERY POUND CAKE
### Yield: 1 Bundt cake to serve 12 to 16
*This pound cake recipe will fill 3 molds (8 ounces each). It is nice in the heart mold.*

1 cup butter, softened
½ cup vegetable shortening
3 cups sugar
6 eggs
2 teaspoons vanilla
2 teaspoons amaretto or orange juice
3 cups flour
1 teaspoon salt
¼ teaspoon baking soda
1 cup sour cream

- Preheat oven to 325°. Spray a Bundt pan with vegetable oil and dust with flour.
- Beat together the butter, shortening, and sugar until mixture is light and fluffy.
- Beat in eggs, vanilla, and amaretto.
- Stir together the dry ingredients, and add half to butter mixture.
- Stir in half the sour cream.
- Repeat with remaining ingredients.
- Pour into prepared pan.
- Bake 1 hour and 15 minutes.
- Allow cake to rest in the pan 10 minutes before turning out onto serving plate.

*Vintage metal gelatin molds are fun to collect, decorate your kitchen with, and bake in. Mirro is the name of the company who made copper-colored metal molds in the '50s. The molds come in numerous shapes: hearts, rings, melons, even roosters, and lobsters! And yes, you can bake cakes in them.*

## VANILLA WAFER CAKE
### Yield: 1 Bundt cake

*This cake slices best when it is cold out of the refrigerator.*
*Tightly wrapped, it freezes well for up to 2 months.*

1 cup butter
2 cups sugar
1 tablespoon vanilla
6 eggs
½ cup milk
1½ boxes (12 ounces each) vanilla wafers, crushed
1¾ cups coconut
1 cup finely chopped pecans

- Preheat oven to 275°. Spray a Bundt pan with vegetable oil and dust with flour.
- In a mixer bowl, beat together the butter, sugar, and vanilla until light and fluffy.
- Add eggs, one at a time, beating between each addition.
- Beat in milk.
- Add crushed vanilla wafers, coconut, and pecans. Stir until well combined.
- Pile mixture into prepared Bundt pan.
- Bake 1 hour and 40 minutes.
- Remove from oven and cool cake in pan for 30 minutes before turning out onto cake plate.

THE EASIEST WAY TO CRUSH COOKIES INTO FINE CRUMBS IS TO PROCESS IN A FOOD PROCESSOR. USE THE PULSE BUTTON AND PULSE 8 TO 10 TIMES OR UNTIL CRUMBS ARE FINE. IF YOU DON'T HAVE A FOOD PROCESSOR, PUT THE COOKIES INSIDE A HEAVY PLASTIC BAG AND USE A ROLLING PIN TO SMASH THEM INTO CRUMBS.

## STRAWBERRY CAKE
Yield: 2-layer cake to serve 12 to 14
*This is a lovely cake for Grandma's birthday, a luncheon for graduating senior girls, or a wedding shower.*

1 boxed white cake mix
1 package (3 ounces) strawberry gelatin
1 package (8 ounces) frozen sweetened strawberries, half for cake and half for icing
⅔ cup vegetable oil
½ cup milk
¼ cup sugar
4 eggs

- Preheat oven to 350°. Spray two cake pans (9 inches each) with vegetable oil.
- In a mixer bowl, place cake mix, gelatin, ½ cup of the strawberries, oil, milk, sugar, and eggs.
- Beat 2 minutes, scraping down sides of bowl halfway through.
- Pour batter into prepared pans and bake 20 to 25 minutes or until toothpick comes out clean from the center.
- Allow cake to rest in the pan for 5 minutes before removing.
- When completely cool, frost with Strawberry Icing.
- The top can be sprinkled with coconut, if desired.

### STRAWBERRY ICING

1 pound powdered sugar, sifted
½ cup frozen strawberries, thawed
½ cup butter, softened

- Place all ingredients in a mixer bowl.
- Beat until smooth and fluffy.

*This is a great recipe that my mom made a lot in the '60s!
It is very moist and very pretty to serve.*

## RED CHOCOLATE CAKE
### Yield: two 8-inch layers

½ cup butter
1½ cups sugar
1 teaspoon vanilla
2 eggs
1 ounce red food coloring
1 cup buttermilk
2½ cups flour
¼ cup cocoa powder
1 teaspoon baking soda
1 teaspoon salt
1 teaspoon vinegar

*Because this cake is such a vibrant color of red, it makes a great Fourth of July cake or holiday cake! For a patriotic cake, decorate with blueberries and strawberries. For a festive Christmas cake, top with red and green gumdrops.*

• Preheat oven to 350°. Spray 2 cake pans (8-inch) with vegetable oil.
• Place butter and sugar in a mixing bowl and beat until light and fluffy.
• Add vanilla, eggs, and food coloring. Beat for 1 minute.
• Stir together all dry ingredients.
• Alternately beat the dry mixture and the buttermilk into the butter mixture.
• Beat in the vinegar.
• Pour batter into the prepared pans.
• Bake 25 minutes or until toothpick inserted into center comes out clean.
• Remove from oven and let cool 5 minutes in the pans before removing.
• Cool completely before frosting with Cooked Cream Frosting.

### COOKED CREAM FROSTING

3 tablespoons flour
1 cup milk
1 cup sugar
1 cup butter
2 teaspoons vanilla

• Place flour and milk in a small saucepan and cook,
stirring until thickened. Refrigerate until cold.
• Beat together the sugar, butter, and vanilla.
• Add cooked mixture a little at a time, beating constantly.

## PINEAPPLE UPSIDE-DOWN CAKE

3 tablespoons butter
³/₄ cup brown sugar
1 can (1 pound) pineapple chunks, drained (reserve juice)
12 to 14 maraschino cherry halves
1 white or yellow cake mix

- Preheat oven to 350°. Melt butter in bottom of 9 x 13-inch baking pan.
- Sprinkle brown sugar on top of melted butter, and arrange pineapple slices on top.
- Place cherries evenly on top of pineapple chunks.
- Mix up the cake according to package directions, using the reserved pineapple juice as part of the water.
- Pour the cake batter evenly over the pineapple.
- Bake cake 30 minutes or until toothpick comes out clean from the center of the cake (195° on your instant-read thermometer).
- Cool cake 5 minutes and then turn onto cake plate.

*Pecan pieces can be added to this cake recipe.
Place one and one-half cup pecan halves or pieces on top of the
pineapple slices before you pour on the cake batter.*

## PINEAPPLE COCONUT CAKE
### Yield: 1 cake (9 x 13)

2 cups sugar
2 cups flour
2 teaspoons baking soda
½ teaspoon salt
½ cup vegetable oil
2 eggs
1 (#2) can crushed pineapple with juice

• Preheat oven to 350°. Spray a 9 x 13-inch cake pan with vegetable oil.
• In a mixer bowl, stir together all ingredients.
• Beat 2 minutes.
• Pour batter into prepared cake pan.
• Bake 35 minutes.
• Remove from oven and immediately pour on Coconut Topping.

### COCONUT TOPPING

⅔ cup evaporated milk
1½ cups sugar
½ cup butter
1 cup shredded coconut
1 cup chopped pecans

• Place evaporated milk, sugar, and butter in a small saucepan.
Simmer 4 minutes, stirring constantly.
• Remove from heat. Stir in coconut and pecans.
• Pour over hot cake.

*Pouring the hot topping over the hot cake makes
this a moist and gooey cake, almost like bread pudding.*

## INSTANT VANILLA CREAM SAUCE

FOR A DELICIOUS, INSTANT SAUCE FOR ANY CAKE OR DESSERT, MAKE UP A BOX OF INSTANT VANILLA OR WHITE CHOCOLATE PUDDING, ACCORDING TO PACKAGE DIRECTIONS, EXCEPT USE HALF AGAIN THE MILK CALLED FOR. IF YOU HAVE IT, FOLD IN SOME PREPARED WHIPPED TOPPING.

## PINEAPPLE PECAN CAKE WITH BUTTER SAUCE
### Yield: 1 large cake to serve 12 to 16

1 cup sugar
1 teaspoon vanilla
2 eggs
2 cups flour
1 teaspoon baking soda
1 teaspoon salt
1 can (20 ounces) crushed pineapple, undrained
½ cup brown sugar
½ cup coconut
½ cup pecans

- Preheat oven to 350°. Spray the bottom only of a 9 x 13-inch baking pan.
- Combine sugar, vanilla, and eggs. Beat for 2 minutes.
- Stir together flour, baking soda, and salt. With pineapple, add to the sugar mixture.
- Beat 1 minute. Pour batter into prepared pan.
- Stir together brown sugar, coconut, and pecans. Sprinkle on top of batter.
- Bake 45 minutes.
- Serve warm with Butter Sauce.

### BUTTER SAUCE

½ cup butter
½ cup evaporated milk
½ cup sugar
½ teaspoon vanilla

- In a saucepan, stir together the butter, evaporated milk, and sugar.
- Bring to a rolling boil, stirring constantly.
- Remove from heat and stir in vanilla.

## WHIPPED CREAM AND CHERRIES ANGEL FOOD FANTASY

1 prepared angel food cake

*Filling:*
1 package (3 ounces) cream cheese, at room temperature
½ cup sugar
½ teaspoon vanilla
1 cup heavy whipping cream, beaten until very stiff
1 cup miniature marshmallows
1 can cherry pie filling

*Frosting:*
2 cups heavy whipping cream
1 teaspoon vanilla
3 tablespoons powdered sugar

*Chocolate Curls:*
Milk chocolate candy bar

- Slice off top inch of cake and set aside.
- With small knife, hollow out center of remaining cake, leaving a 1-inch shell. (Save pieces for snacking.) Place shell on serving platter and set aside.
- Blend cream cheese, sugar, and vanilla. Fold whipped cream and marshmallows into cream cheese mixture.
- Stir and fold in cherry pie filling.
- Pile into angel food cake shell. Cover with reserved top.
- Beat the 2 cups of heavy whipping cream together with the vanilla and powdered sugar until very stiff.
- Frost cake, making big swirls.
- Use a carrot peeler to carve curls from edges of chocolate bar. Sprinkle on top of cake.

## LAST-MINUTE DESSERT

*You will be so proud when you serve this easy yet luxurious dessert! Make it up to 6 hours ahead and store uncovered in the refrigerator.*

- Keep a baked angel food cake in the freezer. It's great to have on hand when you need a quick dessert.
- Serve with low-fat ice cream, fat-free fudge sauce, or pureed fresh fruit. Top with fat-free whipped topping.

243

## KOOKOO CHOCOLATE CAKE
### Yield: 1 cake (9 x 13)

3 cups flour
2 cups sugar
6 tablespoons cocoa powder
2 teaspoons baking soda
1 teaspoon salt
1 teaspoon vanilla
1 tablespoon vinegar
5 tablespoons vegetable oil
1 cup cold water

- Preheat oven to 350°.
- In a 9 x 13-inch baking pan, stir together all dry ingredients.
- Make 3 wells in the dry mixture.
- In the first well, put vanilla. In the second well, put vinegar. In the third well, put vegetable oil.
- Pour water over all, a little at a time, mixing well after each addition.
- Bake 35 to 40 minutes or until toothpick comes out clean from the center.

### Save the day!

Freeze cooled cake layers when you know you are going to need a cake for a special occasion. Wrap the cooled layers in several layers of plastic wrap, then in plastic bags. Freeze the prepared frosting in a freezer-safe bowl, covered with several layers of plastic wrap. Both can be frozen up to 2 weeks. You can even freeze the cake completely frosted! First, allow the cake to freeze uncovered and then wrap as above. This will keep the plastic wrap from crushing the frosting.

Use 1 cup strong coffee in place of the water for a deeper flavor in this cake!

For Chocolate Mocha Icing, use $\frac{1}{2}$ cup strong coffee in place of milk. Keep a small jar of instant coffee in the pantry for quick flavor additions like these.

# CHOCOLATE CREAM CHEESE CUPCAKES
### Yield: 2½ dozen

*This recipe came from my high school youth leader.*
*It won her a baking contest back in the '60s!*

3 cups flour

2 cups sugar

½ cup cocoa powder

2 teaspoons baking soda

1 teaspoon salt

2 cups water

⅔ cup vegetable oil

2 tablespoons vanilla

2 tablespoons vinegar

- Preheat oven to 350°. Place a cupcake paper liner in each of 2½ dozen cupcake tins.
- Combine all ingredients in a large mixer bowl. Beat 2 minutes. Batter will be very thin.
- Fill cupcake liners half full with batter.
- Top each with 1 tablespoon filling (recipe follows).
- Sprinkle each cupcake with 1 teaspoon sugar.
- Bake 25 to 30 minutes.

### FILLING

1 package (8 ounces) cream cheese

1 egg

⅓ cup sugar

⅛ teaspoon salt

1 package (12 ounces) chocolate chips

Extra sugar for sprinkling on top

- Beat together the cream cheese, egg, sugar, and salt.
- Stir in chocolate chips.
- Place a spoonful of topping on each cupcake. Then sprinkle the tops with the extra sugar.

WHY ADD VINEGAR? THE ACID WORKS WITH THE BAKING SODA AND PRODUCES FOAM WHICH ACTS AS LEAVENING. (A LITTLE CHEMISTRY—ALSO FROM HIGH SCHOOL DAYS!)

## APPLE CAKE
### Yield: 1 Bundt cake

1 can apple pie filling
2 cups sugar
½ cup vegetable oil
1 teaspoon vanilla
2 eggs
2 cups flour
1 teaspoon salt
1 teaspoon cinnamon
2 teaspoons baking soda
1 cup chopped pecans

- Preheat oven to 325°. Spray a Bundt pan with vegetable oil.
- In a mixing bowl, combine apple pie filling, sugar, vegetable oil, vanilla, and eggs. Beat well.
- Combine dry ingredients and stir into apple mixture.
- Pour into prepared Bundt pan.
- Bake 55 to 60 minutes or until a toothpick comes out clean from the center.
- Allow to cool in pan for 15 minutes and then invert onto serving plate.
- Serve with whipped cream or Ginger Maple Butter.

### GINGER MAPLE BUTTER
#### Yield: about 1 cup butter

1 cup butter
½ cup pure maple syrup
2 to 4 tablespoons minced crystallized ginger

- Combine all ingredients and beat well.
- Refrigerate overnight to allow flavors to blend.

## APPLE SPICE CAKE WITH BRANDY GLAZE
### Yield: 1 Bundt cake

2 cups sugar
1 cup butter
4 eggs
3 cups flour
1 teaspoon baking soda
1 teaspoon cinnamon
1 teaspoon allspice
1 teaspoon cloves
3 large cooking apples, chopped
1 cup chopped pecans

- Preheat oven to 350°. Generously coat a Bundt pan with vegetable oil spray. Dust with flour.*
- In a mixer bowl, beat together the sugar and butter. Add eggs and beat well.
- In another bowl, stir together the flour, baking soda, and spices. Add the apples and pecans to this mixture. Toss to coat well. Stir into creamed mixture.
- Pack batter into prepared Bundt pan.
- Bake 1 hour.
- Remove from oven and let sit 5 minutes before dumping onto serving plate.
- Allow to cool. Pour glaze over the cake.

### BRANDY GLAZE

2 cups sifted powdered sugar
1 tablespoon butter
Enough brandy to make a consistency of syrup

- Beat together all ingredients.
- Pour and spread over cooled cake.

*Dusting the oiled baking pan with flour gives an extra non-stick layer to help the cake come out easily after baking. To dust, simply toss 1 tablespoon flour into the oiled pan and knock the pan on your counter to distribute the flour evenly. Turn the pan over the sink and tap lightly to lose excess flour.

A BAKING APPLE IS ONE WITH A SMOOTH, ROUND BOTTOM. EATING APPLES HAVE A POINTED BOTTOM WITH LITTLE HUMPS. THESE APPLES HAVE TENDER CELL WALLS THAT BREAK DOWN WHEN COOKED. COOKING APPLES HAVE MORE STABLE CELL WALLS THAT HOLD UP WHEN COOKED AND RETAIN THEIR SHAPE WHILE BECOMING TENDER.

IF YOU GET READY TO MAKE A RECIPE THAT CALLS FOR COOKING APPLES AND ALL YOU HAVE ARE DELICIOUS APPLES AND YOU CAN'T STOP AND GET TO THE STORE, GO AHEAD AND USE THE EATING APPLES! (LIFE IS TOO SHORT TO WORRY ABOUT THIS!) JUST KNOW THAT YOUR RECIPE WILL BE BETTER NEXT TIME, WHEN YOU HAVE THE COOKING APPLES.

## CREAM CHEESE FROSTING
Yield: frosts one 8-inch layer cake

2 packages (3 ounces each) cream cheese
3 tablespoons butter
2 cups powdered sugar
1 teaspoon vanilla

• Combine all ingredients in a mixing bowl.
• Beat until smooth and creamy.

---

## EASY CHOCOLATE SATIN FROSTING
Yield: frosts 2-layer cake (8 inch or 9 inch)

2 cups chocolate chips
2 cups sifted powdered sugar
$2/3$ cup evaporated milk

• Melt chocolate chips.
• Place melted chocolate in mixing bowl. Add powdered sugar and evaporated milk.
• Beat until smooth and satiny.

---

## VERY BERRY SORBET
Yield: 4 servings
*Use your favorite frozen fruits for sorbet. Just using plain strawberries is fabulous.*
*You can use lemon juice instead of orange juice.*

1 package (12 ounces) frozen mixed, unsweetened berries (not with syrup)
2 tablespoons sugar, or to taste
$1/4$ cup orange juice

• Place all ingredients in a blender.
• Blend, using the pulse button until fruit is chopped very fine and mixture
is smooth but still completely icy.
• Serve immediately or place in freezer until ready to serve.

### A

*Allspice*—A spice that tastes like a blend of cinnamon, cloves, nutmeg, and ginger. Buy whole or ground.

### B

*Baking powder*—A mixture of baking soda and cream of tartar (fast-acting acid) or aluminum sulfate (slow-acting acid) that acts as a leavening by producing bubbles when mixed with moisture.

*Baking powder, double acting*—Baking powder contains both fast-acting and slow-acting acids and therefore produces bubbles when mixed with water and again when heated in the oven. Most baking powders sold in grocery stores are double acting.

*Balsamic vinegar*—An Italian vinegar produced from grape juice and aged over 15 years in oak casks. The extra aging produces an extraspecial, rich, mellow, sweet-sour flavor.

*Basil*—An herb from the mint family that grows as an annual in most climates. Its taste is a peppery, minty licorice. It is the main ingredient in pesto and is used often in Italian cooking.

*Baste*—To brush, spoon, or drizzle liquid over food as it cooks, adding flavor, color, and moisture.

*Bay leaf*—An herb that grows on a tree from the laurel family. Its taste is woodsy, mellow, and it is added to food as it cooks. The edges of the leaf are sharp; therefore it is removed from the food before serving.

*Beat*—To mix by stirring rapidly and vigorously. Often used to put air into cake batter and other mixtures.

*Beau Monde*—A seasoned salt containing celery salt, onion powder, and various other spices.

*Blend*—To mix ingredients together until uniformly combined.

*Bundt pan*—A round tube pan with fluted edges, usually used for cakes.

*Broil*—To cook food by placing it under a radiating heat source.

*Broth*—A liquid made from the long simmering of meat, bones, and/or vegetables. Also called stock.

*Bruschetta*—Toasted Italian bread, topped with garlic, olive oil, and other toppings such as tomatoes, olives, or cheese.

### C

*Caper*—The flower buds of a Mediterranean shrub that are cured in a salty vinegar brine and used for flavoring food or as a condiment.

*Capon*—A rooster that has been neutered before it is eight weeks old and prepared for cooking before it is ten months. Larger than a chicken and with a higher fat content, a capon weighs between 5 and 10 pounds. It has more white than dark meat and is more tender and juicy than regular chicken meat.

*Cardamom*—A spice from the ginger family with a pleasant lemon-ginger aroma and flavor.

*Chili powder*—A blend of ground, dried chili peppers, cumin, and other spices. Its heat depends on the chili peppers used.

*Chutney*—An East-Indian condiment made from fruit, sugar, vinegar, and spices. In the grocery store, it is found in a bottle or jar along with other condiments or ethnic foods.

*Cilantro*—The herbal leaf of the cilantro plant. Used in South American and Oriental cooking. See *coriander.*

*Cinnamon*—Dried bark of a tree, native to India. Usually ground or in curled sticks, it is brown in color and has a sweet, woodsy flavor and aroma.

*Clove*—1. A flower bud from a tropical evergreen tree that has a sweet, warm, woodsy flavor and aroma. 2. In garlic, one of the segments that make up the bulb.

*Cobbler*—A deep-dish fruit pie that has no bottom crust and a top crust of biscuits or rolled pastry.

*Coriander*—The seeds of the cilantro plant. Usually ground and used to flavor foods, it has a fresh lemon-sage flavor and aroma.

*Cream*—The component of milk that has at least 18 percent fat. Heavy cream contains at least 36 to 40 percent fat.

*Cream of tartar*—A white powdery acid that is added to give stability to beaten egg whites and to keep sugar mixtures from crystallizing when cooked.

*Crimp*—To pinch the edges of dough to form a decorative edge on crusts.

*Curry powder*—A blend of sweet and savory spices and herbs, used mainly in Indian cooking.

## D

*Dice*—To cut food into small cubes, about $\frac{1}{8}$-inch square.

*Dutch oven*—A large, deep cooking dish with a lid. Used for roasting in the oven and braising and stewing on the stove.

## E

*Egg wash*—A mixture of egg and water, lightly brushed on bread or pastry before baking to add color and sheen.

## F

*Field greens*—A mixture of salad greens that contains various baby lettuces. Usually bought premixed in the produce department.

*Fillet*—A piece of meat or fish that has no bones, with or without the skin.

*Fold*—To mix a light ingredient into a heavier one by gently transferring the mixture from the bottom of the bowl to the top, using a circular motion with a rubber spatula, spoon, or your hand. The goal is to keep as much air in the mixture as possible.

*Frittata*—Similar to a quiche but without a crust. Cooked either in the oven or on top of the stove.

## G

*Ganache*—A smooth mixture of cream and melted chocolate. Used to fill and frost cakes or as the center for chocolate-dipped candies.

*Ginger*—The spicy, slightly sweet, dried spice often used in baking sweets and Indian cooking.

*Grits*—Corn kernels, dried and ground.

## H

*Hash*—Shredded and cooked potatoes, meat, or other foods. Usually fried crisp in a skillet.

## I

*Instant-read thermometer*—A thermometer designed to be inserted into cooking foods. It gives a reading within 10 seconds and is not meant to remain in food as it cooks.

*Italian seasoning*—A packaged blend of oregano, basil, rosemary, and other Italian herbs.

### J

*Jalapeno*—A moderately hot, small green chili pepper.

*Jicama*—A root vegetable with white flesh that is crisp and crunchy with a sweet mild flavor. Mostly used raw in salads.

### K

*Kielbasa* (kil-bah-sah)—Polish sausage made from pork or beef with garlic, spices, and herbs.

*Kitchen twine*—White, medium-weight string used to tie food together while cooking.

*Knead*—To work dough with a machine or hands to develop gluten and produce a smooth texture.

### L

*Leaven*—To cause cooking foods to rise by adding air bubbles.

*Loaf pan*—A rectangular pan used for baking bread, usually 9 x 5 x 3 inches.

### M

*Marinade*—Flavored, seasoned liquid in which meat or other foods are soaked in order to tenderize or add flavor or color.

*Marinate*—To soak food in a marinade.

*Marjoram*—A leafy herb with a flavor similar to oregano.

*Mince*—To chop food into tiny pieces.

### N

*Nutmeg*—The seed of a tree native to the East Indies with a warm, sweet flavor.

### O

*Oregano*—An herb similar to marjoram, used often in Italian and Greek cooking.

### P

*Paprika*—A red spice with a warm, pungent flavor that can range from mild to hot. Used often in Spanish and Hungarian cooking.

*Parchment paper*—Heavy paper used for lining cookie and baking sheets. Grease and moisture resistant, it is also used for wrapping foods, making disposable pastry bags, and forming envelopes in which fish or other food can be baked.

*Parsley*—Bright green, leafy herb with a fresh, peppery flavor.

*Pastry bag*—A cone-shaped bag made of plastic or parchment paper with a small hole at the tip end. It is filled with frosting and then squeezed, forcing the frosting out the tip to form designs on cakes or desserts. It can also be filled with smooth, soft food such as pudding or mashed potatoes and used to fill cream puffs or make decorative designs.

*Pastry tips*—Cone-shaped metal inserts for pastry bags. The small end is cut in various shapes to create designs when food is forced through it.

*Pilaf*—A dish of seasoned rice and other grains. The rice is usually sautéed first and then simmered in liquid until tender.

*Pimento*—A mild red pepper, usually roasted, peeled, and marinated in oil.

*Poach*—To simmer meat or other food gently in liquid.

*Poppy seeds*—Tiny black seeds of the poppy that have a delicate nutty flavor. Used in breads and salad dressing.

*Preheat*—To allow a heat source, usually an oven, to arrive at its correct baking temperature before adding the food to be cooked.

*Primavera*—Food or dishes garnished with vegetables. In Italian, the word means springtime.

*Proscuitto*—Nonsmoked, salt-cured, well-seasoned Italian ham. Usually sold in paper-thin slices.

## Q

*Quesadilla* (keh-sah-DEE-yah)—Entrée or hors d'oeuvre consisting of flour tortillas filled with cheese, beans, salsa, or meat—or a combination of all. Served warm with sour cream and hot sauce.

*Queso* (keh-soh)—Spanish for cheese.

## R

*Reduce*—To simmer a liquid without a lid, causing it to lose moisture through evaporation. Usually used to make sauces more flavorful and concentrated or to thicken a sauce.

*Roast*—Verb: To bake food in dry heat, without covering and without adding liquid.

Usually used to cook meat, poultry, potatoes, and other vegetables.

Noun: A cut of meat that is not tender enough for broiling and is intended for roasting or braising.

*Rosemary*—Pinelike, evergreen herb with a fresh pine flavor and aroma. Used often in Italian cooking. Long life when cut fresh for centerpieces.

*Roux*—A blend of equal amounts of flour and fat used to thicken sauces and soups. The fat coats the starch granules in the flour and keeps them from sticking together and causing lumps. When cooked until dark, the roux develops a nutty flavor and loses its thickening power. Used often in Creole and Cajun cooking.

## S

*Sage*—An herb with gray-green leaves and a musty, woodsy flavor. An important ingredient in turkey dressing and stuffing. Available dried, rubbed, or fresh.

*Sauté*—To cook food quickly in a flat pan on top of the stove using a small amount of fat.

*Sauté pan*—A wide pan with high, straight sides and a long handle, used to sauté food.

*Savory*—An herb from the mint family with the flavor of thyme and rosemary.

*Scallions*—Another name for green onions.

*Seize*—When food becomes lumpy and hard. Mainly used to describe chocolate when it is overheated or when a small amount of liquid is accidentally added, causing it to form lumps.

*Shallot*—A member of the onion family. It is smaller than most onions and has a more delicate, refined flavor. Especially good when used in seafood dishes.

*Shred*—To grate food, such as cheese, fresh ginger, or citrus peelings into thin slivers. Usually done on a grater. Cooked meat can be shredded using two forks to pull it apart.

*Sift*—To run dry ingredients through a fine mesh to blend and aerate.

*Simmer*—To cook liquid at a low temperature, just below a boil but with small bubbles forming.

*Skim*—To use a flat spoon or ladle to remove fat or foam that forms on top of soup or sauces as they cook.

*Soft peaks*—Used to describe beaten egg whites when a spoon or beater is lifted. The peaks should curl slightly and not be pointed.

*Sorbet*—A frozen dessert made with fruit, fruit syrup, egg whites, and sweetener.

*Soufflé*—A dish baked in a container with high, straight sides. Beaten eggs are a main ingredient, causing the mixture to rise and puff and be light and airy.

*Springform pan*—A round baking pan with removable sides. Used for making cheesecake and other food when you want the sides to show.

*Steam*—To place food on a rack or perforated metal basket over but not touching simmering water, allowing the water's steam to cook the food.

*Stew*—Verb: To cook food, covered, in liquid either on top of the stove or in the oven. A slow method of cooking which produces moist, tender food.

Noun: A dish that combines meat and vegetables and is simmered slowly until the meat is tender and flavors are well combined.

*Stiff peaks*—Used to describe beaten egg whites that have peaks that are pointed and firmer than soft peaks.

*Stock*—Broth made from the long simmering of meat, bones, and/or vegetables. Another name for broth.

*Stockpot*—A deep cooking pot used for making stock or large amounts of soup or other food. A lid is used for soup but not for making stock.

*Stuffing*—A mixture used to fill the cavity of turkeys, rolled meats, pasta, or other pliable food. It can also be cooked separate from the food with which it is served. Another name for dressing.

## T

*Tarragon*—An herb with a slight licorice or anise flavor. Often used with chicken.

*Tart*—A pie without a top, usually baked in a pan with straight sides; it can also be baked on a flat sheet by pinching up the pastry around the edges.

*Tart pan*—A pan with straight sides, often with a removable bottom.

*Thicken*—To cause a liquid to become denser by adding flour or other starch or by cooking uncovered to evaporate some of the moisture.

*Thyme*—An herb with a woodsy flavor similar to sage and cloves. Often used in turkey stuffing.

## V

*Vanilla*—A spice used to accent and heighten other flavors in cooking. Available in powder, as dried beans, or as a liquid extract.

*Vidalia onions*—Onions grown in Vidalia, California, which are very sweet and juicy.

*Vinaigrette*—A thin sauce made from oil, vinegar, and seasonings. Used mainly on salads and cold vegetables.

## W – Z

*Whisk*—A cooking utensil consisting of thick wire bent and joined at the handle. Used for whipping ingredients to make a smooth mixture or for whipping air into whipped cream or beaten egg whites.

*Zest*—Noun: The very thin, outer layer of citrus fruits, which contains the oil of the fruit. Verb: To use a knife or utensil to grate zest from citrus.

### Sandwiches

### Sauces and Spreads

### Seafood

### Soups

### Stuffing

### Vegetables